DAVID STONE LIBBEY

HE WAS

PENOBSCOT

"If there is anything that I pride myself on, above my skill as a still hunter, it is my entire and absolute truthfulness."

David Stone Libbey (*Penobscot*)

"*Penobscot* knows the Maine country as well as any man living, and what he may write will be sure to be intelligent and authentic."

Editor of *Forest And Stream*, March 1880

A

Burnt Jacket Publishing

Classic Release

BURNT JACKET MOUNTAIN - MAINE

DAVID STONE LIBBEY

HE WAS

PENOBSCOT

by

Tommy Carbone, PhD

inspired by the book

DAVID LIBBEY

PENOBSCOT WOODSMAN AND RIVER-DRIVER

by

FANNIE HARDY ECKSTORM

1907

and now with writings from David Stone Libbey

DAVID STONE LIBBEY - HE WAS PENOBSCOT

BURNT JACKET PUBLISHING EDITION

Newly added interior illustrations, and photos from the collection of Tommy Carbone, or as otherwise noted.

Author of new material and edition editor, Tommy Carbone.

Use of all newly added material (text, footnotes, and photos) from this book, other than short passages for review purposes or used within quotations with proper attribution, requires prior written permission be obtained by contacting the publisher at info@tommycarbone.com. Thank you for your support.

Public domain Civil War images are courtesy of the National Archives.

Other public domain images are from *Forest and Stream*, 1800s issues, or as noted.

- Civil War letters from David Libbey are courtesy of David M. Rubenstein Rare Book & Manuscript Library at Duke University.

- Lumbering photos courtesy of Josh Swan.

- Cover photo, courtesy of **Cheryl Derico (*cderico photography*)**.

20221206-5.25.8.0-ISPK

ISBN: 978-1-954048-14-0

Burnt Jacket Publishing

1. Maine woods - 2. Penobscot River - 3. Logging - 4. Expeditions and Adventure - 5. Memoir - 6. American History – 7. Hunting and Fishing. – 8. Woodsmen – 9. 19th Century History - 10. Lumberman – 11. Maine History - 12. Biography - 13. River Driving - 14. Civil War

www.tommycarbone.com

DAVID STONE LIBBEY

August 22, 1828 - December 6, 1904

Age 76

The portrait was taken before 1882 and was
provided by David Libbey to be included in the book
– The Libby Family in America 1602 – 1881, by
Charles T. Libby, 1882, (pg. 306 facing). In the
Libby family genealogy numbering utilized in that
book, David Libbey is 6-6-1-5-2-6.

A MAINE LUMBER CAMP

This picture is of a lumber camp on Frost Pond. The bunkhouse building shown would have been typical of those in the Maine woods.

(From, *The Northern*, September 1921.)

CONTENTS

Books from Tommy Carbone

The Lobster Lake Bandits
Mystery at Moosehead

The Elephant Mountain Gang
Mystery at Maine's Moosehead Lake

I AM Penobscot – A Maine Novel

Woods and Lakes of Maine - Annotated Edition:
A Trip from Moosehead Lake to New Brunswick in a
Birch-Bark Canoe

Hubbard's Guide to Moosehead Lake and Northern Maine
Annotated Edition

Exploring the Maine Woods
The Hardy Family Expedition to the Machias Lakes

Growing Up Greenpoint:
A Kid's Life in 1970s Brooklyn

The Penobscot Man – Life and Death on a Maine River

EDITION PHOTOGRAPHS

"Let others frame their creeds — mine is to work;
To do my best, however far it fall
Below the keener craft of stronger hands;
To be myself, full-hearted, free and true
To what my own soul sees, below, above;
To think my own thought straight out from the heart;
To feel and be, and never stop to ask:
'Do all men so? Is this the world's highway?'
To look unflinching in the face of life
As eagles look upon the noon-day sun;
To cut my own path through primeval woods;
To lay my own course by the polar star
Across the trackless plains and mountains vast;
To seek, not follow, ever till the end.
And for the rest — bare-handed have I come
Into this world, I know not whence nor why.
Bare-handed and alone and unafraid,
With heart of fire and eyes that question still,
Will I go forth into the wide Beyond,
As went the men who bore my blood of old
To Eblis or Valhalla nothing loath."

- - - - -

Eckstorm also included this verse as a preface to the last essay written by her father, Manly Hardy, for Forest and Stream, in 1911, printed in, 'Katahdin, Pamola & Whiskey Jack – Stories & Legends from The Maine Woods,' Burnt Jacket Publishing, 2021; as well as in her book, 'The Penobscot Man.' Periodicals of 1902 and 1903 attribute this verse to poet and historian Sharlot M. Hall (1870-1943). The editor finds it peculiar that Hall's name was not included in any of Eckstorm's uses of the verse. The verse is now in the public domain.

INTRODUCTION

In 1907, Fannie Hardy Eckstorm paid tribute to the Man and the man, David Stone Libbey. He was a Penobscot Man, as well as a man she wanted to immortalize for his person. More than this, David Libbey was "Penobscot." Not only did he drive logs on the East Branch of that most wild river of Maine, making him one of thousands of Penobscot men, but he signed his frequent contributions to *Forest and Stream* (and other periodicals) with his signature pen name, *Penobscot*. Whether he was writing from Maine, Canada, the Adirondacks, Nevada, or San Francisco, he shared his knowledge of hunting, wildlife, and the outdoors with the readers. By signing his essays, *Penobscot*, readers knew where he was from, for he was proud of his river, and the entire region of Maine referred to by that name. It is a vast area of the State of Maine where woodsmen consider all bordering land on one of the branches of the Penobscot River to be Penobscot territory, whether in the county by that name, or not. With no small coincidence, Penobscot County is where from a young boy, until his death, David Libbey built his homesteads. He was Penobscot from his calk boots to his hat.

When Eckstorm published her book, it was a small volume of one hundred and ten pages, printed in large line spacing, and in the popular pocket size of easy reading books of the period. Since it was based on a journal of a single man, it did not garner as much interest as her prior river-driver book, *The Penobscot Man*, a book in which she honored multiple men of the river through her skill in storytelling. The reason for the book being based on a singular man is because David Libbey led a life she chose to exemplify for his character and how he stood out among the river-drivers of Maine. To this new book about David Libbey, the reader will find new content, annotations on the writing, as well as, essays from the pen of Libbey himself. It is with great satisfaction to release this book about the life of Maine pioneer David Stone Libbey.

Although Eckstorm knew David Libbey personally, she chose to base her writing mainly on his journals, which were provided to her from his family, without elaborating on her friend's life with details she surely had at her disposal from her own, as well as her father's memory. The publication, printed three years after Libbey's death, likely became a wonderful keepsake for the Stone and Libbey descendants, friends of Libbey, and those interested in Maine pioneer history. Even though the original issue was a book of few pages, it was a critically important work as it documented history, a way of life in the northern rural districts of Maine, and the adventures of one man who left his family behind and took an opportunity to travel across the country to California and Nevada in the late 1870s.

Why Eckstorm originally kept her writing to the limited journal notes was likely due to a couple of factors. Certainly, based on Eckstorm's friendship with David Libbey, coupled with her knowledge of the Maine woods, she could have expanded on his journal. However, she chose to only add general commentary on the ways of this Maine woodsmen, river-driver, and American pioneer. Since this book was originally published in 1907, in the shadow of, *The*

Penobscot Man, she might have been considering some of the critical reviews she received on that book. It is hard to say whether this is so, but twenty years later she took to task the reviewers who claimed she had written fiction.[1] Possibly she decided to stick strictly to the writings as they appeared on the pages of Libbey's journal to not have the book claimed as fiction. This is unlikely, as she wasn't one to shy away from criticism. She once prodded her father, Manly Hardy, to expound on his stories, to which he replied, "I didn't want to make the broth too thick." In this book, not taking her own advice, she left much for the reader to discover about David Libbey in the clear consommé she published.

Of the writings in the journal, Eckstorm wrote, "A thousand tales and one lie buried in these journals, which now no magic may recover; but though our extracts must ever be from the briefest records, which are seldom the most interesting, even these reveal the ability, the uprightness, the worth of David Libbey. His daily records have become his fittest memorial." Of what I have come to label, *Eckstorm clues*, in that quote there are two. Clue one was about the 'lie' she discovered or was told about, and the second seems about the loss of the journals. It is unknown what happened to the journals that were her source for the book, and probably more journals existed, for Libbey kept records of his days for a half a century. The clue about magic being required to recover the journals may indicate something of a destructive nature had occurred to them.

---

[1] See, *The Penobscot Man – Life and Death on a Maine River*, Burnt Jacket Publishing, (2022).

The next discovery of what became of some of Libbey's writings occurred nearly one hundred years after the Eckstorm book was published. In 2003, Joanne E. Brogan discovered a selection of letters Libbey wrote to his wife Mary during his time as a soldier in the Civil War. Joanne was married to Jerre D. Holbrook (born Guilford, Maine, 1935) who was David Libbey's second great grandson, descended from daughter Flora (1858-1925, married to John M. Holbrook). The letters were discovered in an unlikely place, far from Maine in the collections of the Duke University Rare Books library. Upon contacting the university, they kindly forwarded a file which allowed me to transcribe selections of the Libbey letters into this new book.

What is most interesting is that many of the dates on the transcribed letters occur between the dates of the journal entries Eckstorm used for her book with little overlap. We know Libbey wrote during his months with the infantry; yet, Eckstorm only included brief journal notes from that period of his life. This may indicate that she did not have these letters to review during her writing process. So, as to what happened to the original journals, and how the letters arrived at Duke University, is a mystery. The trail, it seems, died with Eckstorm; for the lie she mentions and the reason for needing magic are not included in the broth.

Eckstorm often left room for reader discovery in her writing, a technique she sometimes used to protect the friends she was writing about. It is unlikely this book was short as a need to protect anything of what Libbey had written, for his life was one of a model citizen of the 1800s. Whereas, in other of her subjects, Eckstorm may have figured the knowledge was commonplace, or the stories were well-told at the time. By way of an example, I give the story she relayed in the vicinity of Grand Falls on the Machias Lakes excursion she took with her father in 1891:[2]

"We took time to view the Grand Pitch from the dam both above and below and also crossed the stream to the left side where there is a great, square, out-hanging rock, which some poor witling undoubtedly either has named, or will name, the Devil's Pulpit. Let it be named Joe Mitchell's Rock, for here it was, in full view of the magnificent panorama of the river, the falls and the mountains below, that old Joe used to have his camp and his eel-pots, and here was enacted that laughable story with which many an audience has since been entertained, of Joe Mitchell's eels and Stickney's cow."

Now who was Stickney? And what does his cow have to do with eels? In the essay, she does not say. Why?

Her own journal notes hold the rest of the tale, and it is there we find the following, told to her most likely by her father:

Early in the seventies (1870s) Joe Mitchell and his family were at that very rock on the Passadumkeag, catching and salting eels. One day Stickney's cow

---

[2] See the chapter, *Grand Falls and Spawnook*, in, *Exploring the Maine Woods – The Hardy Family Expedition to the Machias Lakes*, Burnt Jacket Publishing, (2021).

wandered across the bridge, got at a barrel of smoked eels and gorged herself so that she died.

Stickney demanded the price of the cow.

Joe listened gravely, then said, "Mis'r Stickney, your cow been eating my eels,"

"Yes."

"Spos'n my eels gone your cow, been eat it! Your cow eat'n by my eels, I pay for cow. Sposn'n your cow come my eels, been eat it my eels your cow, then you pay for it eels!"

But Joe got no pay for his eels.

The entry does not say if Stickney received any money towards his cow. There really was no particular reason that she did not include the full story in her published essay. It could have been Stickney and Mitchell were still sore over what transpired, maybe she didn't have enough space in her article, or the story had been told so many times in the Maine woods, it was common knowledge. The best conclusion I can make is that her including the details on the death of the cow didn't fit with the positive narrative she was telling in that particular essay, in which the poor cow gets an honorable mention. When Eckstorm made a broth, she usually put in just enough to get her points across, and no more.

In Eckstorm's writing about David Libbey, there was a different constraint to deal with – that being the physical size of the book the publisher was looking for in the "True American Type" series. Otherwise, the editor believes she would have surely included some of his other writings and maybe additional facts about Libbey, for she herself noted the limitations in space permitted from the publisher.

We must also note, that while the north Maine woods, whether above Moosehead Lake, or east of Enfield, are expansive regions, the location of the Passadumkeag River near where Stickney's cow stuck her nose in a place she should have left alone, also has a connection to the Libbey family, one of tragedy, for which I will leave for the reader to discover within these pages.

Whatever Eckstorm's reasons for being brief, this small book about Libbey is now supplemented with writings from his own pen so you may better know the man who was known to so many as, *Penobscot*. While Eckstorm's broth was thin, her clues, allowed me to locate several of Libbey's essays to include in this release. His stories are wonderful reading for those who love the outdoors, wildlife, and nature. Alongside, *The Penobscot Man*, this book with the added material provides a glimpse into the life of a Maine woodsman.

Even if the original was a small volume, I found Eckstorm's tribute to Libbey fascinating. However, this new book with the additions, serves as evidence for exactly what Eckstorm wrote about in her treatise on the man; that this atypical lumberman and river-driver from Maine was well-traveled, well-read, and well-respected by those who understood the ways of the outdoors. In, *The Penobscot Man*, Eckstorm wrote of Libbey, "(he was one of Maine's) thoroughbred woodsman and waterman, one of the most notable of our hunters, who, going to San Francisco, took a place in a stationer's store and handled paper by the quire and arranged perfumery on the closet shelves; and from there to the deserts of Nevada, in the seventies, when it was rough there, where he set up mining machinery and met western bad men, and he unarmed and unruffled made them behave themselves."

Libbey didn't have the opportunity to attend many years of formal schooling, and yet he learned a great deal about literature through his love of books. During an interview with Libbey's son, Charles, he told Eckstorm, "I went to father's memory as to a book for anything I wanted; he opened to the page and read it off; and I never thought of the book being all his own, to be lost with him." We are not afforded with all David Libbey knew, or what he told others, or even all of what he wrote down. But maybe this small volume on his life, and a few of his own essays, will give the reader an idea of what this particular Penobscot man was like and who he was.

I doubt David Stone Libbey would have thought his journal jottings would have made for an interesting book. And, the entries read alone, probably would not be, as he was not one to write long passages in his journals. It was only after the short passages arrived in the talented hands of Eckstorm, that his journal became a book.

Of his published essays added to this edition, his writings were clear, concise, and trustworthy. He was one of the most respected hunters in Maine during the second half of the 1800s. Libbey fished, hunted, trapped, drove logs down unforgiving rivers, dug and transported custom ship knees, and found time to mostly self-educate himself and amass a large library of books. When questions about the Maine woods were raised in periodicals, such as *Forest and Stream*, Libbey could be counted on to contribute his expertise.

In one exchange on the topic of 'panthers in Maine,' Manly Hardy wrote in a letter to *Forest and Stream*: "Dave Libbey, who writes under the name of 'Penobscot,' is certain that he once fired at a panther, and there is no more honest man living than Dave Libbey; but he didn't see the animal very clearly, and missed, and while Dave (I know him very well) undoubtedly thought he saw and shot at an actual mountain lion, it is unreasonable to suppose that in all these years only one mountain lion has been in the Maine woods, and Mr. Libbey is the only hunter that has seen one."[3]

Putting this exchange and debate on the existence of panthers roaming Maine in the mid-1800s aside, the letter from Manly Hardy is important because these two men were friends. Manly Hardy was an expert woodsman, and one of the most experienced fur traders in Maine at the time. The two men respected one another, had mutual acquaintances, found one another trustworthy in the ways of the woods, and their names were synonymous with experts on the Maine outdoors – a point the editors of *Forest And Stream* made many times over the years when referring to either of the men.

The life of David Stone Libbey was certainly not typical of most Maine woodsmen of the 1800s, and Eckstorm alludes to her purpose of breaking a singular stereotype of the 'lumberman' and 'river-driver,' with her spotlight on his career, personal hobbies, and his family life. However, he wasn't the only woodsman who she felt transformed when

---

[3] See, *Katahdin, Pamola, & Whiskey Jack – Stories and Legends from The Maine Woods*, Burnt Jacket Publishing, 2021.

leaving the woods to go to town. In other writing, she was quick to explain how she observed a good number of these men quickly change out of their woods clothes, and even alter their character, once they left the woods. Libbey was documented as a prime example, maybe an outlier, but an example nonetheless, of a woodsman, lumberman, river-driver, hunter, who also was an inventor, and one of Maine's first well-known, and widely respected, writers on the Maine outdoors.

My purpose in releasing this book, with the added information, is to preserve the writings of Libbey as a part of Maine history. The book is a complement to the stories told in, *The Penobscot Maine – Life and Death on a Maine River*, a book in which Libbey contributed his knowledge, albeit following the first publication. While there are a multitude of books about the logging days of old, Libbey was more than a river-driver and woodsman, and this book tells a life story beyond those two occupations. Libbey left a legacy of which his family, and all of Maine can be proud. His writings give us a specific person to think of when we look back on the lives of early Mainers who carved out a place in the forest and made a life worth living.

David Libbey served his country when he answered the call for service during the Civil War. His letters and conviction show he was proud to go, but he also did not spare writing of the hardships he endured and the suffering he witnessed. When David left to serve, he was thirty-six years of age. Others his age, with responsibilities on their farms, paid substitutes to go in their place. Eckstorm wrote of a story in *The Penobscot Man*, where Black Sebat would have gone to service in place of someone else, for a large fee, if only the recruiting officer would have made him a Colonel to start out. Libbey made no such bargain. He marched. He fought. He came home. With the discovery of his surviving letters, this edition provides the reader with more detail from this time in his life.

In writing every single one of the books I've released, there has always come as a complete surprise some connection that I was unaware of when starting the writing process. This book was no different, and the pleasant surprise occurred in a most visual way. For more than twenty years, my evening commute took me through an intersection in the town of Scarborough, Maine. In 2021, a new sign appeared declaring that very location, Libby Corner. The placement of the sign coincided while I was researching David Stone Libbey, who descended from immigrant John Libby, a settler in Scarborough at Black Point.

The extended Libby Family of New England has for decades been preserving the family history. Through their efforts the sign was placed at that corner in recognition of family ancestors who lived and operated a stagecoach station at that location. In fact, members of the Libby family had lived near the intersection from the 1700s until 1987. During the research for this book, the John Libby Family Association, has been a wonderful source of information. The editor would like to thank Allen E. Humphries, the Association Corresponding Secretary (as of 2021) who, within a few hours of an email, provided the editor with information about the Libby family. Allen also made the introduction to Joanne Brogan, the discoverer of the Libbey letters mentioned earlier. The work of the extended Libby family is commendable for keeping their history alive with reunions, books, and events. Additional information is available on the family website (www.libbyfamily.org).

Readers may be wondering why Libbey spelled his name with an 'e,' and the family Association, and the sign at the corner, is spelled *Libby*. The spelling variations were documented by the family historians in 1882. The conclusions were that early generations rarely left any documents to show how they had spelled their name, or they were indifferent to these minor variations. A full treatment of the various spellings, of which nine were noted, is found in the book, *The Libby Family in America*.[4] The spelling David Stone used, as Libbey, is shown clearly in the signed picture later in the book. On the gravestone in Newport Maine for his father, Asa (1786-1854), it is spelled Libby.

You will read that one of David Libbey's means of making a living was the digging of knees. This work goes on even in the modern day, a skill that provides custom timber work for craftsmen. In my research for this book, I came across Mr. Josh Swan. Josh most willingly provided images of his work for this book. As I am someone who struggles to dig out a garden bush, just thinking of the work required to dig a hackmatack tree out of the ground is exhausting.

The cover photo for this book was taken by photographer Cheryl Derico. Fittingly for a book about David Libbey, the image is of the waters of the West Branch of the Penobscot River. Cheryl traveled all the way from Utah and was driving the dirt roads of northern Maine when she captured that beautiful scene of the river. Cheryl loves exploring this

---

[4] Several volumes have been published, and at least one was available in the Scarborough, Maine library. Also available to order from the family website as of 2021 (libbyfamily.org).

wonderful state and I am so appreciative of the images she shares. Find her work online for some beautiful photos.

For those who enjoy reading and learning about Maine history as much as I do, I trust you will find this book engaging and interesting. It is a book of true facts, from a true American type, a fabric of a man who served his family, his State, and his Country.

With the added material in this non-fiction book, the broth is now a little thicker. Since David was such an interesting pioneer of Maine, and had many pioneering woodsmen friends, people who should be well-remembered, I have also released an historical fiction novel covering the time period with David Libbey as a main character. While that story is not a strict following of the timeline of Libbey's life, the hope is that a new generation will come to discover the pioneering spirit, adventure, and well-rounded life of the Maine woodsman and river-driver.

As always, I am interested in hearing what readers think about my books and the subjects. Please find me on social media to let me know if you enjoyed this book about *Penobscot* - David Stone Libbey.

Tommy Carbone

Greenville, Maine

January 2022

ON THE PENOBSCOT RIVER

(From, *The Northern*, 1922.)

FANNIE HARDY ECKSTORM

(1865 – 1946)

FANNIE HARDY ECKSTORM, 1888
Photo taken the year of her college graduation.

Image courtesy of Special Collections, Raymond H. Fogler Library, University of Maine

Fannie Pearson Hardy Eckstorm was born on June 18, 1865, in Brewer, Maine to Manly Hardy and Emmeline Wheeler Hardy. She was the oldest of their six children and attended the public schools in Brewer, Maine and Abbot Academy (Andover, MA). In 1888, she graduated from Smith College (North Hampton, MA), was subsequently employed as the superintendent of schools in Brewer, and for a time worked in the book department of the D.C. Heath Publishing Company in Boston.

In 1893 she married Rev. Jacob A. Eckstorm of Chicago. Seven years later, following the passing of her husband, Fannie Eckstorm and her two children relocated from Providence R.I., back to Brewer, Maine.

Throughout her life, Eckstorm studied Maine Indians, folklore and natural history. It was an area she knew well, based on her experiences with her father in the woods and her personal acquaintance with the Native Americans and woodsmen.

In 1886 she became an associate member of the American Ornithologists Union, the first woman admitted as such. Before graduating Smith College, she co-founded the college chapter of the Audubon Society. Her interest in birds would be a lifelong pursuit, from which she published two books, *The Woodpeckers* (1901) and *The Bird Book* (1901).

She had a deep interest in documenting Maine folksongs and woods songs, and in collaboration with others, two books resulted from her efforts, *Minstrelsy of Maine* (1927) and *British Ballads from Maine* (1929).

Eckstorm had many other community interests, among them, she was a founder and vice-president of the Folk-Song Society of the Northeast, a founding member of the public library in Brewer, and was an honorary member of the Maine Historical Society. Through her association with the local Penobscot Indians, many of who were friends of her fathers, and her grandfathers, she studied and documented Native American culture. Her interest was in preserving their history, their way of life and how they shaped Maine.

She wrote three books on the subject:

- Of Indian Place-Names of the Penobscot Valley and the Maine Coast (1941).
- Old John Neptune and Other Maine Indian Shamans (1945).
- The Handicrafts of the Modern Indians of Maine (1932)

Eckstorm also wrote for magazines such as *Forest and Stream*, *Sprague's Journal of Maine History*, *The Northern*, *The New England Quarterly*, *The Atlantic Monthly* and other publications and newspapers. Her knowledge was well respected by readers and she was never one to shy away from controversy in dealing with facts in her writing, or correcting others. The style of her writing is genuine and her documenting of Maine history has been trusted for over a century.

On December 31, 1946 Fannie Hardy Eckstorm passed away. She had been residing in the same home in Brewer since moving there in 1900.

1907 EDITION BOOK COVER

DAVID LIBBEY

PENOBSCOT WOODSMAN

AND RIVER-DRIVER

(Editor's Collection)

THE LOGGER'S BOAST

THIS ballad follows the life of a Maine lumberman and river-driver, who retires to become a story-teller. David Stone Libbey was such a man. He was known to be a talented singer, captivating storyteller, and excellent writer.

Come, all ye sons of freedom throughout the State of Maine,
Come, all ye gallant lumbermen, and listen to my strain;
On the banks of the Penobscot, where the rapid waters flow,
O! we'll range the wild woods over, and a lumbering will go;
And a lumbering we'll go, so a lumbering will go,
O! we'll range the wild woods over while a lumbering we go.

When the white frost gilds the valleys, the cold congeals the flood;
When many men have naught to do to earn their families bread;
When the swollen streams are frozen, and the hills are clad with snow,
O! we'll range the wild woods over, and a lumbering we will go;
And a lumbering we'll go, so a lumbering we will go,
O! we'll range the wild woods over, while a lumbering we go.

When you pass through the dense city, and pity all you meet,
To hear their teeth chattering as they hurry down the street;
In the red frost-proof flannel we're encased from top to toe,
While we range the wild woods over, and a lumbering we go;
And a lumbering we'll go, so a lumbering will go,
O! we'll range the wild woods over while a lumbering we go.

You may boast of your gay parties, your pleasures, and your
    plays,
And pity us poor lumbermen while dashing in your sleighs;
We want no better pastime than to chase the buck and doe;
O! we'll range the wild woods over, and a lumbering we will
    go;
And a lumbering we'll go, so a lumbering will go,
O! we'll range the wild woods over while a lumbering we go.

The music of our burnished ax shall make the woods resound,
And many a lofty ancient Pine will tumble to the ground;
At night, ho! round our good camp-fire we will sing while rude
    winds blow:
O! we'll range the wild woods over while a lumbering we go.
And a lumbering we'll go, so a lumbering will go,
O! we'll range the wild woods over while a lumbering we go.

When winter's snows are melted, and the ice-bound streams are
    free,
We'll run our logs to market, then haste our friends to see;
How kindly true hearts welcome us, our wives and children too,
We will spend with these the summer, and once more a
    lumbering go;
And a lumbering we'll go, so a lumbering we will go,
We will spend with these the summer, and once more a
    lumbering go.

And when upon the long-hid soil the white Pines disappear,
We will cut the other forest trees, and sow whereon we clear;
Our grain shall wave o'er valleys rich, our herds bedot the hills,
When our feet no more are hurried on to tend the driving mills;
Then no more a lumbering go, so no more a lumbering go,
When our feet no more are hurried on to tend the driving mills.

When our youthful days are ended, we will cease from winter
    toil,
And each one through the summer warm will till the virgin soil;
We've enough to eat, to drink, to wear, content through life to
    go,
Then we'll tell our wild adventures o'er, and no more a
    lumbering go;
And no more a lumbering go, so no more a lumbering go,
O! we'll tell our wild adventures o'er, so no more a lumbering
    go.

There have been many singers who have recorded versions
of this song, most all with varying lyrics, but of the same
theme. Additional ballads were included in, *The Penobscot
Man – Life and Death on a Maine River – Annotated Edition,*
Burnt Jacket Publishing *(2022)*.

THE RIVER-DRIVER

SO far as I can observe river-driving did not breed a type. The hunter was a type—you could tell him at a glance; the lumberman was a type—he was easy to distinguish; but I cannot recall that after he had shed his peculiar clothes, the river-driver was a marked man. It was the life they lived the rest of the year, rather than the few weeks on the drive, that classed them as types. With most of them, river-driving was a metamorphosis rather than a profession. The more reckless either died young or reformed, the more intelligent and ambitious worked into other occupations and became head boatmen, head lumbermen, millowners, or land-owners. I have known a few to enter the learned professions and come out doctors and lawyers.

As a trade river-driving is not without a parallel. After a long trip through the southwest forty years ago, my father came back and delivered an ultimatum.

"Come to think it out," said he, "a cowboy is only a river-driver on horse-back."

Anyone who understood the old cowboy can understand the river-driver as he used to be. A log—the old, big log—was as much a brute beast as any steer, and acted like one. It could do anything a steer could do, and much worse when it piled up in those huge jams that had to be cleared out at no matter what risk.

The similar work bred men of like type, who worked hard and played hard, but not always judiciously, and then went back to work again.

The River-Driver is taken from Fannie Hardy Eckstorm's journal. She also used these words in the chapter *'Tis Twenty Years Since*, which she added to the re-issue of *The Penobscot Man* in 1924.

David Libbey, while he was a river-driver and an expert boatman, he certainly was not of any 'type,' or what we today might think of as a stereotypical lumberman of the woods.

Libbey enjoyed singing, he worked at his craft of searching out timber for ship's knees, he was an inventor, a collector of books, a writer, and an expert woodsman. One has to wonder where he found all the time to enjoy such passions and provide for his family. This book will provide us with a glimpse into the type of life he led.

RUNNING A LOG

THE LIBBEY FAMILY

LIFE can hardly be sane and sweet, foursquare in all its human relations, and be more austerely simple than this Maine woodsman's. Yet his was not a life of negations and renunciations. He met all the demands of son, husband, father, brother, friend, citizen, and soldier, and yet had time for self-education, for aesthetic culture, and for the exercise of a talent by no means meagre. He was, moreover, the true type, however much he might surpass the average, of a class of men distinguished for their honesty, courage, loyalty, versatility, and singular ability to cope with emergencies.

David Libbey was known among his mates as an expert woodsman, a bold and skillful waterman, and a great hunter; he was known elsewhere as a man of literary gifts and varied attainments; but perhaps no one outside the small circle of his intimates knew the whole man, the quality of his mind, the breadth of his interests. The diaries upon which this sketch is founded are the only minute and satisfactory record of a woodsman's life of which I have any knowledge, and they show a man no less remarkable for character than for diversified experiences. In his journals, in which there is hardly a day's break in fifty years, we meet him as hunter and machinist, head-boatman and carpenter, miner and timber-moulder, farmer and clerk, foundry-man and soldier, naturalist and writer, ranging from Atlantic to Pacific, spending the winters of half a century in the woods. It is a wonderful record, but no eulogy could be so eloquent as the confidence with which his family permitted a stranger to them to examine those records of fifty years without blotting a word, or folding a page, or prohibiting the publication of a syllable.[5] A thousand tales and one lie buried in these journals, which now no magic may recover; but though our extracts must ever be from the briefest records, which are seldom the most interesting, even these reveal the ability, the uprightness, the worth of David Libbey. His daily records have become his fittest memorial.

The thoroughbred Maine woodsman has behind him at least three generations of pioneer ancestors. David Libbey had six. Therefore, to dismiss his origins with the bare statement that he was the son of a British soldier would be misrepresentation. He was an American yeoman of the purest stock.

John Libbey, the immigrant, arrived in Maine about 1635, settled permanently at Black Point in Gorges' patent.[6] Years ago the family historian estimated that from him and his two wives over three hundred thousand individuals had originated.[7] For three generations his descendants colonized

---

[5] Eckstorm is noting she was a stranger to the Libbey family members, but she herself, and her father, Manly Hardy, knew David Libbey for many years.

[6] Named for the Somersetshire Englishman, Sir Ferdinando Gorges, a man who never set foot in America, but who financed a 1606 expedition to what would eventually become the State of Maine. Fort Gorges in Casco Bay is named for him.

[7] The family historian at the time Eckstorm is referring was Charles T. Libby. He began compiling extended family

the coast between Cape Elizabeth and Great Boar's Head.[8]
The fourth generation scattered more widely. About 1764
Samuel Libbey of Epsom, New Hampshire, removed his
family to Machias, Maine, and later to St. Stephen, New
Brunswick, though not until his son Eben was old enough to
select as his future wife Lydia Young of Gouldsboro, Maine.
Thus, though their son Asa Libbey, of the sixth generation
from the immigrant, was born on British soil, he came from
the purest possible American ancestry. No doubt Asa Libbey
intended to remain a British subject; for, after getting what
education he could, going in the woods a little, going to sea
a little, and learning ship-carpentering, he settled upon
soldiering and at the age of twenty-four enlisted in the British
army. He served two years. But when the War of 1812 called
him to fight the land of his forefathers, he deserted without
delay and came across to Maine. It was not discreet to pursue
his trade of soldiering; there were equally good objections to
his sailoring on the high seas just then; he therefore fell back
upon his other trade and turned his skill with adze[9] and
broad-axe to the shaping of masts and house-timbers.

No one knows precisely how or when Asa Libbey came
to the Penobscot. A younger sister of the future Mrs. Libbey
alone preserved the tradition. Little Aunt Edgerley, eight
years old, remembered his coming to her father's late one

---

genealogy in 1879, the year of his high school graduation. He
published the first impressive volume of family names in 1882.
[8] Near Hampton, New Hampshire.
[9] An adze is a tool with an arched blade, perpendicular to the
handle. It is used to shape wood, and in other sizes as a hoe for
agriculture.

evening, tall and fine, in knee buckles and short clothes, with ruffled shirt and ruffles at the wrists. From this brave array we suspect that little Aunt Edgerley was not enough in Sister Abigail's confidence to know whether this was the first time they ever saw each other.[10] On the sixth of December, 1815, when he was twenty-nine and she eighteen, Asa Libbey married Abigail Cutler Stone, the daughter of David and Deborah (Chesley) Stone, of Milford, Maine, people of staunch Massachusetts stock who came to Maine with the great immigration after the Revolution.

The Libbeys were always pioneers. Many times a newly married Libbey had cut a swath of pine and planted his log house in the wilderness. This Asa Libbey did also, settling at what is now Edinburgh on the west bank of the Penobscot River. Needless to say, the region was a wilderness then; today, ninety-one years after Asa Libbey brought his bride there, the town can muster but eleven voters, with no exempts.[11] Probably the clearing and the log cabin were prepared in advance, as was the custom, though the land was left full of stumps and untamed. Little enough cleared land, too, it is likely, raising only a trifle of English grass for the cow, a few potatoes, a few pumpkins, some beans and buckwheat, and a little Indian corn. "Pine" was the word in those days, as magically delusive as "gold" became later, and a good broad-axe man could not afford to waste his time farming.

---

[10] David's Aunt Edgerley, sister to his mother Abigail.

[11] Two-hundred and five years later, according to the 2010 census, the town of Edinburgh had a population of 131 persons.

The Libbeys lived in Edinburg and the adjoining town of Howland from 1815 until 1840.[12] All their children were born and two of the daughters died while they were living there. David Stone Libbey, the sixth child, and second and last son, was born the twenty-second of August, 1828, in a log house by the river's bank, child of pioneers, with six generations of pioneers behind him.

What such a childhood meant is hard to imagine; but boys so brought up were men at fourteen, resourceful, strong, inured to hardship, unflinchingly brave. Lydia White, David's sister, has told me of his pluck, persistency, and courage when a boy. He was afraid of nothing. A favorite sport, with boys and girls alike, was to take a slab of driftwood, point it at the ends, and propelling it by an edging, to steer boldly out upon the Penobscot, there no mean stream, in unruffled confidence that barks guided by Providence come safe to port.[13]

Schools were infrequent then. One ten or twelve-weeks' term, in summer or in winter, was their year's allowance. Mrs. White remembers that once in summer, while playing on their way to school, David fell into the Piscataquis just below the dam. Though three years younger and much frightened, she pulled him out by the heels. She also recalls winter evenings by the open fire, mother and sisters knitting, her father shaving cedar shingles, and the low log cabin filled with the fragrance of the wood. Then from the shavings and the "cedar-hair" curled about her father's feet, she would

---

[12] Near the intersections of the Piscataquis River, Seboeis Stream, and the main branch of the Penobscot River.

[13] An 1800s version of a paddle-board.

feed the blaze that David, sitting in the opposite jamb of the fireplace, might have better light while doing his sums.

And when his task was done, the father would set aside his shingle-horse and read aloud from "Paradise Lost" or from the romances of Sir Walter Scott.

The Libbey's home was the ordinary two-room log cabin of the pioneer, the children sleeping in the spare room or in the loft above, the living-room containing the bed of the parents, the loom, the spinning-wheel, the shingle-horse, the cradle, the dining-table, and all the pots and pans of the numerous family. None of their neighbors had more, few had as much. For here were always tallow candles for the father to read by, — which was a luxury; and here were all of Asa Libbey's books.

These were the household wealth, the silent teachers of David Libbey and his sisters, correcting by sweet influences the errors of their speech, attuning their ears unconsciously to the noblest cadences of their native tongue. One ceases to marvel how this backwoods family of half-schooled children grew up to write such prose and verse as several of them did write, when one learns of Asa Libbey's books. Comforts they lacked, but culture they had.

"How he got the first of his books we do not know," say his daughters, "but we think that he must have brought them back from St. Stephen when he and mother went over to visit while Joseph was a baby." That was in September, 1820. Such a visiting, too, of the young wife upon her husband's kin!

She had then three children. Sally and Mary — who, by the way, went to San Francisco as early as 1850 to become two of the city's first school-teachers — were left with their mother's parents;[14] the five-months-old Joseph she took with her on a journey of a hundred and ten miles through unbroken woods.

We see now that Asa Libbey must have come into Maine this way, else he would never have known that old Indian route to Calais by way of the Passadumkeag. And what a flight that was through the wilderness, up the wide Passadumkeag meadows, across blue Spawnook, over the two-mile carry past the Grand Falls, up the winding Main Stream, across the long Dobsy Carry, and down the great wild lakes of the St. Croix system! And even as the mother hugged him to her breast, the eyes of the infant Joseph looked upon the roaring waters of the Grand Falls where he was to meet his death.[15]

On Dobsy Carry, three miles and forty rods of liberal woods' measure, Abigail Libbey had to leave the baby while she helped her husband in carrying the canoe across. When they came back, hours after, the baby could not be found, and it was not until they were on the point of despair that they

---

[14] This seems to be at odds with the Family genealogy volume and may be a typo in the original text. Sally did not leave Maine. Mary was joined by her much younger sister, Emma in California, and the two of them were teachers.

[15] Joseph would drown twenty-two years later on the Passadumkeag near Grand Falls, east of Saponac Pond. This is in the Downeast region of Maine where, with her father and Jot Eldredge, Eckstorm took a three-week long trip to the Machias Lakes. Their trip is described in *Exploring the Maine Woods – The Hardy Family Expedition to the Machias Lakes*, Burnt Jacket Publishing, (2021).

discovered the lost infant.[16] The modern mother cannot understand to go visiting required the leaving a helpless infant alone for hours in a trackless forest full of bears and wolves; but pioneer necessities required such risks. I have heard of other cases than this of a baby being lost in these great woods.

When they came back from their visit, Asa Libbey brought his beloved books, stout volumes covered with leather. He must have loved books to carry them on his back across those nine miles of carries. His English school-books undoubtedly came back now, probably also his Pope and Milton and some of Scott's works. His daughters mention by name *Peverilof the Peak, St. Ronan's Well, Guy Mannering, The Lady of the Lake*, Bulwer's *Night and Morning* and *The Last Days of Pompeii, Thaddeus of Warsaw, The Scottish Chiefs, Pickwick Papers,* Thompson's *Seasons,* and Gray's and Young's Poems as among the books in their home when they were children. In this collection, their father owned all of Scott except *Ivanhoe* and *Woodstock,* which he secured later; and, as they appeared, he bought most of Bulwer-Lytton's and Dickens's works.

The father's favorite was *Paradise Lost.* He could repeat long sections of it, and he delighted to read it aloud. His wife used to be very impatient over this, avowing her inability to see anything admirable in the poem, and protesting that she did not like the metre. Probably she thought there was more sound than sense to it, or else she disapproved Master

---

[16] At five months of age, the infant Joseph must have crawled away from where he was left, or the parents had trouble finding the location they had left him. The notes do not elaborate.

Adam's discourses upon woman-kind, concerning whom he seems to have had more self-sufficiency than knowledge.

It is clear how David Libbey acquired the style which marks his writings, for great models are better than many masters. An intimate friend of a younger generation says: "He was familiar with the Bible, Shakespeare, Longfellow, Tennyson, Byron, Browning, Holmes, Scott, and all the poets and novelists of any note. He was not only familiar with these authors but could render verbatim many long cantos and selections. He seemed to get the exact meaning, and many pieces I knew by heart sounded different rendered by him. I think he was more partial of late years to Bret Harte and Kipling."[17]

We should not fail to notice that this household was skilled in music. Asa Libbey possessed an excellent voice and sufficient knowledge of music to write original airs for words he composed himself. He had taught singing-school also, and had at hand a large repertory of songs which were a great source of winter entertainment to the young folk of Rowland. David Libbey once began a list of the songs he himself knew, and the tally, incomplete, reaches almost three hundred titles. He once wrote out for me from memory an English ballad of fifty verses which his son says he had sung but twice in thirty years.

---

[17] In an illustration of 'thin broth,' Eckstorm does not name this friend of David Libbey.

A Brief Summary of David Libbey's Family Tree

David's grandfather, Eben Libby (ab.1760 - 1818) was born in Epsom, N.H. He married Lydia Young (b - 1843) of Gouldsborough, ME. The couple had twelve children. At nineteen, his family moved to St. Stephen, New Brunswick.

Asa Libbey (1786-1854), David's father, was born in St. Stephen. Asa returned to the United States and married Abigail Cutler Stone. They lived in Edinburg until 1833 and then moved to Howland until 1840. Asa was a river driver and lumberman. In 1840, they moved to Greenbush and he subsequently was involved in farming. The family history provides for the following ten children and noted husbands.

1. Sally A., b. 6 Dec. 1816, in Edinburg; d. 23 Oct. 1835.

2. Mary S., b. 1 Nov. 1818; married 23 June 1853, in Marysville, Cal., to Louis H. Bonestell. Mary was one of the earliest teachers in San Francisco. Louis H. Bonestell was a 49er. They had three children. (Louis had relocated from New York State to California with his brother, John, for the gold rush. John married Jovita Ferrer.)
   2.a – Blanche Bonestell
   2.b – Chesley Knight Bonestell
      2.b.i – Chesley Knight Bonestell, Jr. (1888 – 1986) who became a famous artist and illustrator.
      Incidentally, the name Chesley was the maiden name of Abigail Cutler Stone's mother, Deborah Chesley, of Milford, Maine.
   2.c – Cutler Bonestell

3. Joseph E., b. 1 May 1820; was drowned 29 April 1842, while river driving on the Passadumkeag River near Grand Falls.

4. Nancy D., b 12 Jan. 1823; married 20 July 1845, Isaac Young; d. 10 May 1863.

5. Almira B., b 29 March 1825; d. 4 Oct. 1836.

6. David S., b. 22 Aug. 1828; married 23 March 1857 to Mary A. Young of Greenbush, ME. Moved to Newport, ME in 1870. They had three children
    6.a Flora, b. 2 July 1858; m. 13 Sept. 1879 to John M. Holbrook. The couple had eleven children.
    6.b Alice, b. 23 June 1866.
    6.c Charles Truman, b. 2 Nov. 1868.

7. Lydia A., b 2 Feb. 1831; married 24 Aug. 1851, m. James M. White.

8. Emma M., b. 5 Dec 1833; married Sept. 1867 in San Francisco to John Truman Bonestell, brother of sister Mary's husband.

9. Sarah E., b. 11 Dec. 1836; unmarried.

10. Abba M., b. 14 Aug. 1840; married 15 June 1862 to Charles Young, brother to sister Nancy's husband.

Volumes of the Libby Family Genealogy books.

The initial volume of this family genealogy was published in 1882. It is a most impressive catalogue of the descendants. Copies are available at the Scarborough, Maine library.

DAVID LIBBEY'S CHILDHOOD

THERE are but two authentic records of David Libbey's childhood. In *Forest and Stream* for April, 1879, he tells of the capture of his first trout.[18]

"It has been a little more than forty years since the writer, then a 'bare-foot boy,' drew his first trout (a three-pounder) from the sparkling waters of the Seboois just where it joins the Piscataquis. And what, O disciples of split bamboo, braided silk, invisible gut, and singing reels, do you suppose was the tackle used on that momentous occasion? A black alder pole, cut on the spot, to which was attached a discarded band from the busy spinning-wheel, which was then found in almost every dwelling in the state. Fastened to this by a black linen 'gange' was a small but coarse-wired and blunt-pointed hook with a side-bend, which we called a 'curbed' hook, being as near as we could get to 'Kirby.'[19] I had caught a small chub with this primitive tackle, and with a small boy's cruelty was amusing myself by spinning him through the water, when the tempting bait caught the hungry eye of a magnificent trout, which had probably just turned in from the

---

[18] This is only an excerpt of the first paragraph of the essay Libbey wrote in 1879. It was submitted during his time in San Francisco. He signed his essay, *Penobscot*. The full letter is included in a chapter of this edition. This story was from a time when he was about ten years of age.

[19] Charles Kirby, whose shop was in Harp Alley in London, set a new quality standard for fishing hooks with his design in 1650. Many types of hooks are sold on his original design principle today.

river to begin the ascent of the stream. With a lightning-like rush he gorged both fish and hook and then commenced the 'tug of war.' Ye Gods! What a commotion was created in that quiet eddy by the desperate and futile struggles of the noble fish to escape from the cruel hook, and my equally vain and frantic efforts to lift him from his native element! Finding my strength unequal to the task of lifting him with that awkward and unwieldy pole, I adopted the tactics of an elder brother who was overmatched by a big eel; and shouldering my pole, I marched inland, dragging my prize ingloriously up the sandy beach, the rotten line giving way just as I got him at a safe distance from the water's edge."

In a letter to myself Mr. Libbey gives the other picture of his childhood: —

"My father in his youth was one of the most noted ballad-singers on the river; but the death of his eldest son, my only brother, who was drowned at the Grand Falls of the Passadumkeag while river-driving, April 29, 1842, and taken out of the water on his twenty-second birthday, May 1st, changed the whole current of his life. He was never known to sing a song after that awful shock. I was thirteen the previous August, and too young to remember the greater number of his favorite songs, like *The Union of St John's,* *The Cruel Mother-in-law,* and a score of others. When a child I had a phenomenal voice, and the river-drivers used to hire me to sing.[20] At seven years of age it was ruined, as I

---

[20] This fact of Libbey's singing to river-drivers must have been of great interest to Eckstorm, for at this time in her life she was already compiling ballads of the Maine woodsmen that she would eventually publish in a book. Libbey may have started out singing to the river-drivers, but he would eventually become

had strained the vocal cords, and from that time till my voice changed at manhood, I never even *whistled* a tune. Then it partially returned; but although I could sing better bass than any tenor of my acquaintance, and better tenor than any bass, yet a good bass could beat me at the one and a good tenor at the other; so my voice was very unsatisfactory to me."

A pretty picture, this of the little boy, standing with closed eyes and upturned face among the river-drivers gathered about their evening campfire, singing to them like a lark, while the tattered, sunburned men listen eagerly and pay him well. Where can one find the mate to it short of Bret Harte's miners to whom he read —

"While the whole camp, with 'Nell' on English meadows.
Wandered and lost their way."[21]

I have dwelt purposely upon these minor matters. President Eliot, in his life of John Gilley, expounded the economic side of the life of the Maine pioneer of eighty years ago.[22] Here is evidence that there was intellectual refinement

---

a cook's assistant, and subsequently one of the best river-drivers to handle a batteau in Maine.

[21] Bret Harte (1836-1902), was an American short story writer who wrote fiction featuring miners, gamblers, and other stories focusing mostly on the California Gold Rush era. Libbey's sister, Mary, would marry Louis Bonestell, himself a 49er who left New York State to stake a claim.

[22] Charles W. Eliot (1834-1926) was president of Harvard University for 40 years. He wrote the story, John Gilley in 1899, and it was published in *The Century Magazine*; the book form followed five years later. See inset.

in the same period and condition. With nature appreciated, with the best of books for companions, and music a constant solace, real culture was attainable even in backwoods cabins. And across it all the red thread of tragedy: what of the father, who, after his eldest son was drowned, "never sang again?"

"TRUE AMERICAN TYPES"

Vol. I. JOHN GILLEY: Maine Farmer and Fisherman, by CHARLES W. ELIOT.

Vol. II. AUGUSTUS CONANT: Illinois Pioneer and Preacher, by ROBERT COLLYER.

Vol. III. CAP'N CHADWICK: Marblehead Skipper and Shoemaker, by JOHN W. CHADWICK.

Vol. IV. DAVID LIBBEY: Penobscot Woodsman and River-driver, by FANNIE H. ECKSTORM.

Price, each, 60 cents, *net*; by mail, 65 cents.

AMERICAN UNITARIAN ASSOCIATION
Publishers, Boston, Massachusetts

This 1907 advertisement for the books of the "True American Types," lists Mainers David Libbey and John Gilley among four men for which books were written. Gilley as part of the family of light keepers on Baker's Island, and Libbey a pioneer family of the Maine woods.

The Gilley family made their life on Baker's Island which is considered part of the Cranberry Isles, just off the coast of Mt. Desert Island. The son, John, was a seaman and fisherman who began his labors transporting Maine cobblestone to Boston. He bought a farm on Sutton's Island where he farmed and fished for sustenance. He was a town official on the island, for what little that was worth. Late in life, he made some small fortune selling land, to nonother than the college president who was buying up land with other prominent families that would spur Bar Harbor and Acadia National Park. At the age of seventy his business was delivering, each day regardless of weather, milk, eggs and vegetables from Sutton Island to North East Harbor, a point on Mt. Desert. Gilley's end at 74 years of age came much like the end of David Libbey's life. As Libbey's story is to be told in this book,

> *and the small book about Gilley is widely available, the editor will leave those endings for the reader to discover. Eckstorm's point to be made here is that Gilley's life was the subject of hard economics, while making due; and likewise, with Libbey, who all the while also pursued intellectual endeavors and adventure far from home.*
>
> *A river-driver and a Maine fisherman may not have been a particular type of man, but we can be sure, Libbey and Gilley were both from the stock of "True American Types" of the 19th Century.*

In 1840 Asa Libbey removed his family from the west to the east side of the Penobscot and settled in Greenbush. Here he had one hundred and sixty acres of land, though only five were under cultivation. Here, for the first time in their lives, his children lived in a framed house. Mary, Joseph, Nancy, David, Lydia, Emma, the second Sarah, and Abba were the children now living.[23] Up to this time Asa Libbey had worked in the woods and on the river; but now, being fifty-four years old, he retired to be a farmer, leaving his sons to succeed him in his former and more profitable occupations.

After Asa's retirement Joseph stepped forward to be the main support of the family; but only two years later, in 1842, while breaking a jam on the Grand Falls of the

---

[23] It is not clear which daughter Eckstorm is referring to as the first *Sarah*. In the book of the Libby Family history, the first-born daughter was named Sally (1816-1835). The daughter, Sarah E., was born Dec. of 1836. It could be that the first born was Sarah, and not Sally as noted in the family lineage book; however, it was David Libbey himself who provided the family information to the family historian, so that is unlikely.

Passadumkeag, he was swept under the logs and drowned. Although his comrades caught him and his clothing was stout, the river tore it under their grasp and he was carried, as many another man has been, to a death which no strength nor skill nor foresight could avert. It may have been in part the feeling that his son was his substitute which accounted for the change in Asa Libbey after Joseph's death.

From the time of his brother's death until his first diary takes up the story, there is no record of David Libbey's life except a little bear story, too long to quote, too good to spoil, which he wrote for *Forest and Stream*. It shows that while still a boy he was working as a cook in a lumber camp. On this occasion the bear did most of the hunting, and David "vowed if ever he reached camp with a whole skin to become one of the most exemplary cooks on the river."[24]

Illustration from, *Forest Life and Forest Trees: Comprising Winter Camp-Life Among the Loggers, and Wild-Wood Adventure with Descriptions of Lumbering Operations on the Various Rivers of Maine and New Brunswick* (1851).

---

[24] The noted bear essay is included in this edition as the next chapter.

A BEAR STORY

IN this edition one of two Libbey bear stories is included. The other is left for the interested hunter-reader to discover. This story occurred when David Libbey was about thirteen years of age. His experience to be relayed certainly taught the young hunter a good deal about the behaviors of bears. Libbey was a fast learner and without fear, became one of Maine's most successful hunters.

THE true history of the bears has yet to be written. I believe that naturalists advance two theories to account for their existence through the winter without food. One is that they go into their dens extremely fat, and that this fat is slowly absorbed during the winter, thus sustaining life, and that the bear comes out in the spring in a lean and famished condition. The other theory is that the temperature of the animal's body, instead of being fixed like ordinary mammals, varies with that of the surrounding atmosphere, being always at a point a little above it, consequently when cold weather comes on it is cooled down to such a degree that there is no wasting of the tissues, and the animal remains dormant.

During my first winter in the woods, I officiated as cook to a small crew employed by my father and, as the cooking did not occupy half my time, I used to join the gang in the woods between meals. Coming to camp one afternoon to cook supper I was aroused by the well-known voice of "Old Tigress," a large, black female, famed as a "moose dog" throughout that whole region. I knew by her bark that the game was at bay, and as she never deigned to notice anything small, I was all excitement in a moment. Hurrying into camp I seized my gun, and hastily providing myself with some buck shot, I ran down to where the dog was barking, scarcely twenty rods from camp. On reaching the spot I was greatly disappointed to see her standing alone and barking at a hole under the roots of an enormous hackmatac stub.[25] Going up to her I was about to reprimand her for fooling me, when I caught sight of a lot of freshly picked boughs sticking out of the hole. I had listened to too many hunters' stories not to know at a glance what that meant. Only one animal in Maine has sufficient intelligence to stop up the mouth of its den with boughs after going in. Hurriedly drawing out the fine shot with which my gun was loaded, and putting in a charge of buckshot, I stepped up to the roots of the tree, and, boy like, thrust the muzzle of my gun into the mouth of the den and pulled the trigger. The charge merely grazed the bear's thigh, cutting a shallow groove in the fat with which it was overlaid. It was a very cold day in the latter part of December, but I never saw an animal any less dormant than that bear!

With one movement of his powerful hind legs he forced himself through the aperture at the mouth of his den, throwing the earth outward in every direction, and in much less time than I have taken to tell it he stood before me, one of the largest bears ever seen in that country. It was the first I had ever seen, and his enormous size, so much larger than I had ever dreamed of, appalled me; but he was within ten

---

[25] Hackmatack of the *Larix* laricina, known as the Alaskan Larch, American Larch, Eastern Larch, Tamarack, as well as, Tamarack Larch.

feet of me, and I dared not turn my back on him. Coming so suddenly into the strong light seemed at first to blind him, and he stood for a moment motionless, winking incessantly.

The dog, partly between me and the bear, but a little to one side, stood like a statue with hair erect and glowing eyes fixed on those of the bear, which commenced to turn its head slowly from side to side to discover the foes who had so rudely disturbed his repose. As his vision cleared, he caught sight of me, and laying back his ears and opening a capacious mouth well garnished with yellow teeth, with a snort like the puff of a locomotive, the seemingly unwieldly animal bounded at me with the lightness of a cat. With a leap that I can truly say was for life, I placed nearly the same distance between us, as that which first separated us, and, dropping my gun, sprung to the foot of a scrubby spruce close at hand, and began to ascend it with all possible despatch. Fortunately for myself I was not pursued.

Scarcely had the beast's feet landed in the tracks which I had so kindly vacated for them, when the dog, executing a skillful flank movement, fell suddenly on his rear with a fury, which completely turned his attention from myself. This gave me ample time to ascend the tree, from the summit of which I watched the combat below. This, however, was all one way, as it consisted of a scenes of charges by the infuriated brute upon the dog, which did not attempt to bite the bear after the first rush, but contented herself with simply dodging its attacks. After expending his fury in a score of vain attempts to get the dog into his power, he desisted, and, walking toward the den, actually endeavored to re-enter it. Being again attacked by the dog, he turned and once more drove her back, and then sullenly retreated into the forest, closely followed by his tormentor.

As they disappeared, I descended from my perch, and, picking up my gun, proceeded to reload. By the time this was accomplished, my drooping courage had wonderfully revived, and I started on the trail, determined to risk another shot, the hunter's instinct being, even then, strong within me. I soon overtook him, as he turned continually to drive back the dog, which of course rendered his progress slow. When I started, I had made up my mind to advance within twenty feet of the monster so as to deliver a fatal shot, for sure. But the thought obtruded itself, as I came in sight of the huge beast, that my gun might miss fire. I confess that I had not the nerve to go so near. Turning to drive back the dog, he came within thirty paces of me. As he turned broadside to me to continue his retreat, I delivered the charge full at his right shoulder, and a tremendous charge it was, nearly knocking me off my feet. The heavy coat of hair and the thick layer of fat arrested the shot before they could penetrate to a mortal depth; but they wounded him quite severely and roused him to a pitch of fury impossible to describe. The roar of mingled rage and pain which he gave as the shot struck him I shall never forget to my dying day.

When it struck on my ear I instantly sprang for the nearest tree. The brute bounded toward me with a speed no one would have believed him capable of, and although the dog fastened to him before he had made half the distance to the tree, he paid not the slightest attention to her, but swept her along as though she had been a feather, and gained the foot of the tree before I was well out of his reach. But although the dog could not prevent his reaching the tree, she did hinder him from making any attempt to seize me. The bear, indeed, seemed to think he had a sure thing on me, and, turning furiously on the dog, he drove her before him for several rods and again rushed toward me, but the noble brute fastened to the bear as often as he attempted to return to the tree, and invariably ran away from it when he charged on her. Being defeated in every effort to return to the tree, the contest ended as before, the bear slowly retreating followed by the dog. By this time, I had come to the conclusion that bear hunting, as a sport, was not a success, and vowed if ever I reached camp with a whole skin to become one of the most exemplary cooks ever known on the river.

BEARS IN THE MAINE WOODS
(From, *Thomas S. Steele's – Maine Adventures Two Book Collection.* Burnt Jacket Publishing, 2021.)

On again reaching terra firma, I could not, however, resist the inclination to follow the trail for a few rods just to observe the effect of my shot. He was bleeding slowly, and following the trail for a short distance I came upon a sausage-shaped substance nearly two inches in diameter and about six in length, evidently just ejected by the bear, and followed by a stream of fluid as black as ink, which extended for nearly a hundred feet; there must have been several quarts of it. My curiosity was greatly excited. This, then, was the "plug," as the hunters called it, which I had often heard them declare the animal provided itself with before going into winter quarters. I had always supposed it to be a fable; but here was proof positive of its truth. I examined it carefully, and tried to break it in pieces, but it was as tough as copper, and almost as hard, being evidently composed principally of pitch. Since that time I have had opportunities to examine a number by dissection, while in position. It is placed at the extremity of the rectum. It not only fills the passage, but adheres to it perfectly on all sides, rendering it perfectly air-tight. I have always found the intestines empty, with the exception of the black fluid of which I have spoken, which appears to be extremely astringent in its nature. Whether it is secreted naturally, or obtained by the animal from some peculiar plant, I, of course, have no means of knowing.[26] It is

---

[26] With the benefit of 150 years and wildlife biology, the fecal plug is now known to be of intestinal secretions. These secretions include indigestible hairs and bits of den-bedding, such as leaves, twigs, and bark that the bear ingests during hibernation and grooming. All in all, David Libbey proves himself as not only a good writer of a story, but from subsequent

evidently slowly absorbed during hibernation, as it always occurs in less quantities as winter advances. In company with a companion, I once killed one in its den, the 18th of March. It was, I think, the fattest bear I ever saw; a perfect mass of fat inside and out. As the animal would have left of its own volition in a couple of weeks, it will readily be seen that it had not existed by absorption of fat. There is not the slightest doubt but the animal comes out of his den in precisely the same condition in this respect in which he entered it. It is probably equally true that the bear could not exist without this mass of fat which envelops him, as it serves in some mysterious way to perfectly protect the tissues and muscles from any waste. Having served its purpose, it rapidly disappears when the beast leaves his den, and in two or three weeks after that event he is as lean as a rat, and correspondingly voracious.

Perhaps I ought to say in regard to the bear with which I began this article, that he was followed the next day by two of the crew. They tracked the bear a distance of six miles, and killed him in a new den which he had dug for himself. The dog had followed him about half that distance. He proved to be one of the largest ever killed in that part of the country.[27]

---

decades of observation and examination he is shown to be of scientific mind to draw conclusions.

[27] The second bear story from Libbey, titled, Part II can be found in the *Forest and Stream*, August 15, 1878, Vol. 11, No. 2. It is not included here, but the theme is a multi-day bear hunt that the hunter may find of interest.

ADVERTISEMENT FOR RIVER DRIVER BOOTS
(From the year 1900)

Notice the spikes to gain foot hold on the logs.
These were called calk boots by the lumbermen and river
drivers. (Sometimes spelled caulk or cork.)

THE JOURNAL BEGINS

WHEN he was twenty-four years old, David began his first diary.[28] To the stranger, none in the series is more interesting than this brief record. It is a diary of the smallest size, three days to a page, with headings like these:

- Jan. 10. Sacramento City over-flowed, 1850.[29]

- Jan. 11. Dr. Dwight died, 1817. *(As this entry is between two from 1850, the date of 1817 must have been the birth year of the doctor - unknown.)*

- Jan. 12. Packet ship *Ayrshire* wrecked, 1850."[30]

---

[28] As, David Libbey was reportedly born in 1828, and Eckstorm has these entries noted from 1850, he was twenty-two or twenty-three at the time.

[29] The first great flood of the city of Sacramento, which had been built in a flood plain. An interest to Libbey as his sister Mary was living in San Francisco.

[30] The British ship *Ayrshire* ran aground off Squan Beach, New Jersey, in January 1850. All but one of 166 passengers and 36 crew were saved due to a new installation of the "iron life-car" at the location which was hauled between the stranded vessel and the beach by rope.

Nothing shows more plainly than these now trivial dates the barrenness of the pastures that imagination fed in then. The diary runs on with boyish freedom (Eckstorm chooses the next entry from two years in the future): —

- 1852, Jan. 8. Came very near losing what few brains I happen to possess.

- Jan. 9. A meat-bird surrounded me and like to have carried me off.[31]

- Jan. 15. Began a road through a long cedar swamp.

- Jan. 18. Broke two axe handles and made one; so much for working Sunday.

- Jan. 20. Made out to get a hole through that cedar swamp and haul two sticks of Juniper, Clear and devilish cold."

The effervescence of youth is in these inconsequential jottings. Later on he would have told us what it was that so nearly killed him; the ubiquitousness of the Canada jay would have been taken for granted; the axe handles would not have subtended a question of casuistry.

It is a record of hard work, hauling every day four to six big sticks of "juniper," or an average of 3500 feet of pine; yet sometimes the record is the merest whimsey.

---

[31] Canada jay. For a wonderful Eckstorm essay on Whiskey Jack, see, *Katahdin, Pamola & Whiskey Jack – Stories and Legends from The Maine Woods,* Burnt Jacket Publishing, (2021).

Once there is a bit of verse, written prose-wise for lack of space.

> *"May coquettish.*
> *Sometimes pettish,*
> *Smiling often*
> *Through her tears,*
> *In rotation*
> *Yields her station,*
> *And the welcome*
> *June appears."*

Why put that in? It is Youth — an idle day of gentle rain no doubt, and day dreams. It struck his fancy, and there is every evidence that David Libbey had both fancy and imagination in a degree uncommon in a man whose work was hard and practical.

Once there is the entry:

- April 6. Went to Greenfield.

And in a later hand, marked all about with a little cross-hacked fence, is this:

# #

- Number I of an indefinite series. —

"Was it to see you?" I asked *his* wife, seeing that here was romance.

She blushed a pretty trifle.

"No, not me. We were just boy and girl together, and grew up so. That was Jim White; he married Sister Lydia the year before."[32]

# #

---

[32] Sister Lydia married James (Jim) White, August 24, 1851.

So there was romance there, after all: a man goes to visit his brother-in-law and he fences in the record as if to keep the weeds out! But where can one find truer romance than this fifty-year old friendship of man for man? Only the brevity of this memorial justifies writing of David Libbey without also writing of this friend and kinsman, his constant companion in the woods and on the river. "When my brother was drafted," said Lydia White to me, "I lay on the floor and cried all night because brother had to go and my husband was rejected; I wanted them to be together."

In this northern country, one who strikes deep enough to find the heart of us will discover that our finest romances are these friendships of man for man. Wives may be as dear and true as these two were, but they cannot always come first; and the wife herself, obedient to a racial instinct, will hold this tie of friendship as something too fine to be crossed by claim of hers; there are times when she will sacrifice the husband in the service of his friend as resolutely as any heathen woman would.

Once more the little book: —

- 1852, May. Paid $3.50 for a four months old puppy; named him Rolla.

- July 5. Went to Bangor to circus and caravan and theatre twice. Received of D. Dudley, Towne's Fourth Reader and Spelling-book, Smith's Geography, Atlas and Arithmetic.

- July 6. Came back from Bangor. Went to digging knees.[33]

- July 12. Began going to school.

The young man of twenty-four, river-driver, ox-teamster, lumberman, and hunter sits patiently on a cramping school bench through the heat of summer doing sums. This is the one time in his life when we feel inclined to pity David Libbey — because he could have so little of what he was eager to have so much. Probably all his school-days would not more than equal three modern school years. It is known that from thirteen until eighteen he did not go to school at all.

There is but one entry more to be taken from this diary, valuable because it is the only record of any religious crisis in David Libbey's life. After his brother's death his father had become "a chief pillar in the Free Will Baptist Church," but David had as yet made no professions. Now he had evidently been attending meetings held by some itinerant evangelist.

- Oct. 3. Protracted meeting commenced.

- Oct. 11. Came home. Went to meeting. Found one half of the youth converted and the other half trying to be.

---

[33] Digging knees, is the process of digging timber from hardwood, or deciduous trees. The 'knees' are cut, with considerable digging, from the angle between the trunk and taproot. During these years, ship architects would contract for exacting pieces of timber. The blueprint would often be taken into the woods, and the digger would search for trees to meet the required design.

- Oct. 14. Went to meeting. Very much edified by hearing that I was going to the residence of his Satanic Majesty and dragging others with me.

- Oct. 17. Protracted meeting closed.

Here was a youth who needed only the touch of a wise man to realize himself; but the evangelist evidently was not that wise man. David Libbey never joined any church, though later on, in the order of Free Masons, he found an organization recognizing duties both manward and Godward. There can be no question of the reality of his religious life; independent of all forms and ceremonies, free from dogmas and hierarchical dictation, again and again the journals show that he knew a way and walked in it. In his day the ability to be independent without being reactionary is worth observing.

The year 1852 marked the high tide of David Libbey's youth. In it he has that orgy of amusement, "the circus and caravan and theatre twice," in two days, something which his self-denying life never paralleled again; he finishes his schooling, gets him a watch, acquires the dog that stood his friend for fifteen years, and the friend who never failed him in fifty. It is safe to say that this is the year of all his youth best worth recording.

The next year's diary (1853) is scattering and inconsequential; the next three years (1854-1856) he kept no record of events. From this time on the diaries are those of a mature man, who deals in facts without comment. Rarely, except at the end of the year, do we get the personal, intimate touch of this first little book. But how good are the others, too! How full of the life of the woods! How valuable for their minuting of the common events of the woodsman's everyday life!

The only important event in the diary of 1857 is this: —

- March 23. Went to town meeting. Married this evening by Rev. Wm. Doble to M. A. Young.

There is no little fence about this record to keep the weeds out, though daily and yearly he testified how good it is when two dwell together in unity.

Mary Ann Young, the daughter of Henry and Susan (Low) Young of Greenbush, Maine, was of the same pioneer parentage as himself, and was his boyhood's choice. They grew up for each other. It seems hardly proper to lay bare so simple and pleasing a romance, which did not know what it enfolded until it was full blown. Three children came of the union, a daughter born before the war (Flora), and a daughter and a son born after it (Alice and Charles), all of whom married in due season. Before David Libbey's death, fifteen grandchildren had come to gladden and enlarge the family circle.

Perhaps this is the place to speak of the unity of this family group, where not only were parents and children uncommonly devoted, but the brother and his sisters always kept warm the affection of their youth, and the fraternal ties embraced those who married into the family. As the two sisters in California married brothers (Louis and John Bonestell), while two of Mrs. Libbey's brothers (Isaac and Charles Young) married sisters of her husband, the circle was unusually compact. From the West, Mr. Libbey writes often and affectionately of his sisters and their husbands; at home he is rarely found camping or hunting with anyone but his cousins by marriage, Josiah and Bingham Edgerley, and his four brothers-in-law, James White and Isaac, Charles, and Benjamin Young.

Lumbering and hunting were the chief occupations of this group. Moose and deer, they hunted for the meat and the skins, and bears for the skins and for sport. After that first discomfiture by a bear, David Libbey became an excellent bear hunter, though never equal to his brother-in-law, Ben Young. Indeed, since over half a century ago, when Old Jim Lyford of Brownville passed away with three hundred and twenty black bears to his credit, anxious to live until he should have one for every day in the year, Benjamin Young has been the most noted bear hunter in Maine. David Libbey wrote me once of a bear hunt in which both of them were engaged which stands without a parallel.

On the tenth day of December they routed out a very large bear. The weather was intensely cold, six inches of snow, with a crust; yet for sixteen days they followed him, until, the morning after Christmas, with the thermometer thirty-five below zero, they came up with him and killed him after a sharp fight. In all that time the bear ate nothing, living entirely on his fat.[34]

The diary for 1859 shows David Libbey deer-hunting with White, Josiah Edgerley, and Isaac Young. They bring in from two to five deer a day, the total being forty-five deer in a trifle over five weeks, including stormy days and

---

[34] The second bear story. See earlier footnote for publication date.

Sundays. Of course, this was killing for market and in the winter snows, both forbidden today though at that time legal and honorable methods of hunting.

The next winter, that of '59-60, is spent in pursuit of a different kind of game. He is moose-hunting in the northern forests, above the mountain quaintly named "The Traveller," because it seems to keep one company for mile after mile down the East Branch of the Penobscot. It is a record full of exciting hunts, in which men, dogs, and moose fight grim battles in the snowy forests; but the best of them are too long to quote.

The year 1860 opens as with the blare of a trumpet: —

- Jan. 1. Hauled out the old bull moose to Fothergill's.
- Jan. 2. Hauled out the young bull.
- Jan. 4. Two fat bucks.
- Jan. 5. A doe.
- Jan. 7. Two old does.

Two moose and five deer, in eight days, by one man! This is certainly a condensed hunting story. But what a tale might be unrolled from such brevities by one who knew all the facts. Here is another, selected only because it is so brief: —

"Went out to bring in a deer; came across a moose track; followed it ten feet and saw him standing 150 yards distant; shot *seven bullets* into him; broke my gunlock and started to get it mended."

And in the same breath he adds:

"Bo't *Cumming's* 'Five Years in South Africa.'"[35]

It is a far cry from a desperate fight with a raging bull moose in the shaggy forests of northern Maine to lion-hunting on the hot plains of Africa; but the journal proves that the lion-hunter had nothing to teach the moose-hunter about dangerous sports.

A Maine hunter in those days did not pump out seven bullets in two minutes, hit or miss. He had an old muzzle-loading rifle; powder, patches, bullets, were all in different places; he must ram his ball home accurately with freezing fingers; he must take aim at the life. Those seven bullets, therefore, were all sent home to vital spots. But a bull moose, fighting mad, cannot feel his death. Time after time he will charge the hunter, driving him into deep snow. After his seventh ball was fired, the hunter tripped on his snow-shoes and broke his gun in his fall, and the moose almost got him that time. That is the story of the broken gunlock. Did he kill the moose finally? The diary does not say. Sometimes, after a fight lasting for hours, it was the hunter who withdrew, out of ammunition and baffled, leaving the moose the master of his bloodstained yard.

---

[35] Bo't *Cumming's* '*Five Years in South Africa.*' – Bo't is his term for *bought*. Likely referring to the book, *Five Years of a Hunter's Life in the Far Interior of South Africa*, by Scottish Roualeyn Gordon-Cumming (1820-1866).

Those who are curious to know the financial results of a successful winter's hunt may have the memorandum of Libbey's share of the proceeds of the winter of '59-'60:

For venison killed in Nov. and Dec.,
ten saddles	$56.26
2 moose, Jan. 9.	$43.00
9 venison saddles	$35.22
1/3 of twelve moose hides	$12.00
	Total $146.48

"I carried a rifle twelve of the best years of my life for a livelihood, with a score of deer killed squarely by still-hunting at least equal to any in the State," says he, in *Forest and Stream*; yet this winter, one of the best on his records, nets him less than a hundred and fifty dollars, without board, for six months of very hard work.[36]

Hunting was a fall and winter occupation; in the spring many hunters became river-drivers. David Libbey began river-driving at seventeen, for this is a trade to be followed only while one is young and nimble; after they are thirty, so the river-drivers have told me, most men are too stiff and clumsy to go on the logs; they still go on the drive, but in other capacities.

---

[36] In 2022 dollars, this $146.48 is about $4,800. Hardly an exorbitant wage for eight weeks or more of hard winter work all the while camping in the woods. Men in these days had more than one source of income and jobs varied throughout the year.

Of the year 1870 David Libbey wrote me:

"Even then I had drove — that isn't good grammar, but it's good dialect — twenty-five seasons, handling boat fifteen of them."

"*Handling boat*," that is, guiding the batteaus over the falls, is the most responsible and highest paid work on the drive, therefore it is interesting to note the wages received for it in different years.

In 1859 he got $1.25 a day and "found," for river-driving always includes board. In 1860 he got $2 a day.

Thereafter the wages kept rising steadily, until in 1870 he hired for $4.50 a day.[37]

On the West Branch that year a few of the best men got $5 a day; but David Libbey never drove the West Branch.[38]

---

[37] In, *The Penobscot Man – Life and Death on a Maine River*, the editor made note of river-driver wage rates. In 1863, a river foreman by the name of Scott, offered the famous Fowler brothers, $15 a day ($7.50 each) as expert boatman on the stretch of river they knew best between Quakish Lake and Shad Pond.

[38] In 1870, Libbey was 42, and the age when men turned away from the dangerous profession of driving logs. 1870 was also the year, Joseph Attean was drowned near Shad Pond. The fact that Libbey never drove or handled boat on the West Branch didn't make him any less a *Penobscot man*, since he drove the tributaries and the East Branch and many other Maine rivers.

From then on wages fell, until in 1890 they were $2.50 for the very best men, $1.75 for common hands. It should be remembered that this is expert labor, the work very hard and risky, and the day twice the length of the ordinary working day, being commonly eighteen hours of labor, with much night work.

For anyone curious to know how a river-driver chronicles his adventurous days, we may quote from the record of 1860, dignified in its bareness of detail: —

- June 17. Went over Island Rips.
- June 19. Went over Gordon Rips.
- June 20. Went over Piscataquis Falls.
- June 21. Went over Passadumkeag Rips.

- June 23. Went into boom at Oldtown and back home.[39]

- July 5. Bo't *Tennyson's Poems, Worcester's Dictionary, Prince of the House of David.*[40]

---

[39] Libbey's river trip that year was down the Mattawamkeag River. Gordon Falls, are approximately five miles upriver from the joining with the Penobscot. His trip took him down the main branch of the Penobscot River past Brown Islands, Snow Island, and Hersey Island; then past the intersection with the Piscataquis River at Howland and Enfield, Maine.

[40] *Prince of the House of David*, published in 1859 by G. G. Evans, is the story of Christ's years of ministry on earth told by a young Hebrew girl in the form of letters to her father. While it seems David was not devoutly religious as far a church-going man, he read the bible and books about Christ.

This last entry comes as unexpectedly as running out on a gravel-bed.[41] Most people, even among those who know them, imagine that the first thing a river-driver buys is whiskey; the man who prefers Tennyson is not often taken for a river-driver, even by his neighbors.[42]

In those days, river-driving was over about the first of July, and from then until the hunting or lumbering began in October, there was time over and above the intermittent labors of small farming, for another occupation.[43] With David Libbey this was, by preference, the cutting of ship-timber and digging of ship-knees. These are different trades, but they may be carried on together where the growth permits.

Ship-timber is from hardwood, or deciduous trees; whereas the knees are always of hackmatack, here invariably called "juniper." Knees were cut from the angle between the trunk and taproot, and digging them was profitable work. I have been told that "there were times when a man could earn

---

[41] The crunching scrape of gravel on the bottom of a canoe will be familiar to anyone who has run swift water of a river, sometimes being stopped unexpectedly.

[42] In 1983 Port Ellen Distillery offered in it's 'Authors' Series' a 33-year-old single malt scotch named, Alfred Tennyson. Such a scotch may have been more to most river-driver's tastes over a book. However, the editor wonders if Tennyson would have felt this an honor – given the violent nature alcohol played in his young life at the temper of his father.

[43] In the early and mid-decades of the 1800s river driving came to an end earlier in the year as dams were small cribworks and the headwaters were not the large lakes of reservoirs they'd later become once the much larger dams were built.

a suit of clothes in a day — a really good suit, too — by digging knees." Libbey's most extensive "operation" in knees was in the winter of '60 and '61, when, with James White, Charles Young, and Bingham Edgerley, he spent the winter in New Brunswick.[44]

He alone could dig from forty to sixty a week, and he worked over five months. All four men were experienced watermen, and they made their own drive in the spring. It was on this occasion that they twice ran McDougall's Falls, a feat never before attempted by any man.

The journal says merely: —

- Ran McDougall's Falls and filled our boat.

RIPS ON A MAINE RIVER
(From, *The Northern,* 1922.)

---

[44] The reader should imagine the work of digging tree roots through a season of a New Brunswick winter.

It was James White who told me the story in detail.

"We handled boat together nine springs, David and I, and we never swamped one once. But once we filled our boat on McDougall's Falls. The first time we ran there was Sunday. We made up our minds that we could go over those falls — nobody ever had been over.

"We began by taking out our stuff above the falls, and the Province men standing round asked us what we were going to do.[45] We told them that we were going to run those falls. Well, we ran them all right and didn't take in more than a half a pailful of water.

"We had another drive of knees to take down, our rear,[46] and meantime the water fell a foot and a half, which made the falls very bad. When we came along we didn't even run ahead to look out the channel, but put right along. The first time we two were alone; this last time we had Charles Young, who is dead, and Bing Edgerley, who is living, with us, and we ran it on paddles. There was one place where we had to run out around a rock. She dove under and came up full, sweeping everything out of her, and David, who was in the bow, along with it.[47] He caught the side.

---

[45] Province men, the term for Canadians, or more specifically, Prince Edward Islanders. See, *The Penobscot Man – Life and Death on a Maine River,* Burnt Jacket Publishing (2022).

[46] "The rear" of their drive means the final section of timber to float down.

[47] The bow position in fast water is the position of *honor*, or most responsibility. Explained fully in, *The Penobscot Man – Life and Death on a Maine River* (IBID).

"Said I, 'She's full!' And he tumbled in and ran for his place in the bow.

"He yelled 'Keep her straight, don't let her run into the eddy; keep her out in the current!'

"And by keeping her out in the current we made out to get her to shore again."[48]

The stranger calls it a fool's hazard for men with families to take such risks. It is rarely that altogether. Here they were winning laurels for all Penobscot men, as the first to dare do this. And more than that. In those days of the beginning of the war the feeling in the Provinces was very bitter against the States; so that this was a patriot's service.[49]

---

[48] McDougall's Falls are on the Magaguadavic River, sometimes referred to as *Mackadavy* and has the meaning *River of Eels*. In, *The Penobscot Man – (IBID)*, the story *Joyfully* is told from a Hardy family friend about his time river-driving on that river.

[49] Certainly conjecture, but given her experience as demonstrated in her research for her book, *The Penobscot Man*, Eckstorm was probably not far from the mark for the reasons these men ran the falls.

The following images were provided to the editor from Josh Swan. Mr. Swan cuts hackmatack knees that are dug from trees in Northern Wisconsin. These photos give the reader an appreciation of the labor that goes into the cutting of this timber.

Images courtesy of *Josh Swan –*
J. W. Swan & Sons – Boats, Timber, Workshops.

Left: Selected trees, ready for digging.

Right: A knee, at close to three-feet high.

Digging complete.

Knee dug from the ground.

Molded timber shaped into required angles.

Braces ready to be formed to specifications.

A MAN AT WAR

TO this chapter, letters David Libbey wrote home to his wife, Mary, while he was deployed during the Civil War are included with the journal notes from the original book. As noted in the introduction, these letters were discovered at the Duke University library. In most of the letters Libbey appears to write his wife's name as, *May*. Handwriting comparison shows he clearly writes words ending in 'r y' with two distinguished letters. However, in writing to his wife, and even his sister who is also named Mary, the writing appears as 'Sister May,' the 'r' appears to be dropped from the name. Since this is likely his script tendency, the letters are typed here as Mary. Some of the letter entries have been abbreviated and most all have been slightly edited for punctuation.

A number of the lines in the document with the letters are concise, and have the characteristics of David Libbey's journal entries that Eckstorm had published. In his letter dated May 7, 1865, he wrote that his knapsack was stolen, along with all his mail, and other personal belongings, but the section of journal-like entries begin five months earlier in January of that year. The most likely explanation is he sent pages home in installments, so as not to have to carry them from encampment to encampment. In several letters, he mentions he mailed home transcripts and poems.

It is curious that only a few of the journal entries Eckstorm included in the book coincide with the dates of the found letters. This indicates the two sets of records were either unique, and not stored in the same set of materials that Eckstorm was given to use by the family; or only a selection of the journal pages ended up in the Duke University archives. While this is not much of an importance for this book, it may be of interest for those who do further research on David Libbey.

In the original publication, Eckstorm did not dwell on the time Libbey spent at war. First, she had a length constraint from the publisher; second, her book was about the full life of Libbey; and third, she may or may not have had access to the letters Libbey wrote home from the war. As we are no longer constrained by any of these limitations, the writings of Libbey from his own letters are added between that of the original text. His words give the reader not only an idea of the conditions Libbey endured, but also his love of his wife and family. It appears, that no matter his situation, Libbey remained mostly positive, at least in his letters.

WHEN the war broke out David Libbey, as we have seen, was in Canada, and he remained there nearly two years longer; but all the events of the war he followed with the keenest interest, subscribing for a Bangor daily paper even when far up in Canada East.[50] With a wife, mother, and child dependent upon his daily work for their support, it was impossible for him to enlist, although all his friends were going. But when called out by the draft of 1864, he

---

[50] The date most associated with the breakout of the Civil War is April 12, 1861, when shots were fired on Fort Sumter, near Charleston, South Carolina.

responded.[51] On the 1st of October he went into camp at Portland, and was assigned to Co. D, 9th Maine Infantry.

Libbey wrote his first letter home on October 2nd, 1864 from Camp Berry in Portland, Maine.[52] He signed each letter, *Ever Yours, D.S.L.* Selected excerpts are included from the letters.

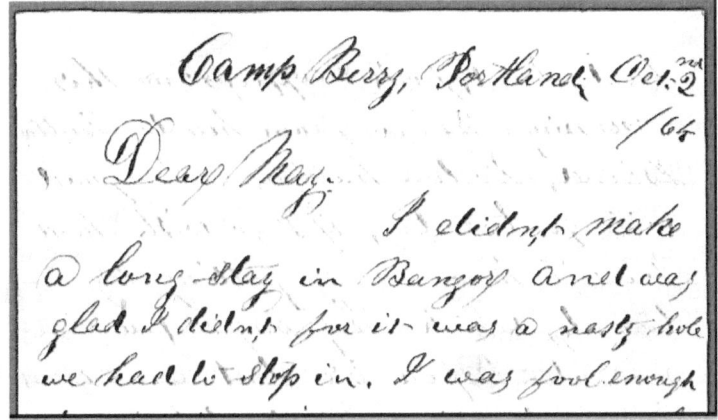

An image of the start of the letter transcribed for this edition.

- - -

- Oct. 2. Dear Mary

I didn't make a long stay in Bangor and was glad I didn't for it was a nasty hole we had to stop in. I was fool enough to report as soon as I got in the city – expecting to get liberty

---

[51] Libbey was 36 years old.

[52] Camp Berry was a Civil War recruitment and training camp. It had its beginnings as Camp Butler located on Mackworth Island in Falmouth in 1861. The camp moved several times and before it was closed in 1866 it was in Ligonia, a portion of what is now South Portland, Maine at Long Creek and the Fore River.

to go out again but I couldn't, so I didn't see about the wool or anything else. I didn't even get anything to eat till dark and then nothing but cold beef, cold water and hard bread; all the coffee being drank up before I got a chance to sit down. I got a seat at the first table the next morning and tried to drink it all up away from the rest of them and hope I succeeded. We didn't get anything more till dark last night then hard bread, pork & coffee, same this morning.

- - -

In the full letter, Libbey relayed he would send home his bounty of $20. The Civil War bounty was the money an enlistee received for signing up for duty; the amount varied according to the time to be served. He wrote, "We go from there to Bedloes Island, Boston harbor. A squad will go Tuesday, if I go with them, you will know it by getting my bounty, which they pay a few minutes before we start an expressman standing ready to take it if you wish to send it home. I will send you the receipt which must be presented before you can get the money."[53]

From Boston, he was transported to Virginia.

- - -

- Oct 7. Gallops Island, Boston Harbor.

Dear Mary,

We came from Portland to Boston in the Portland and NY steamer *Montreal*. It is a nice situation looking out on an old ocean dotted with white sails and green island on one side,

---

[53] This was a misunderstanding in the midst of assignments. Bedloes Island (from the 1600s until 1956) was the name of now Liberty Island in New York Harbor. In his next letter of Oct. 7, he provides the correct name of the fort he arrived at in Boston - Gallops Island, Boston Harbor.

and a distant view of the cities and villages of Massachusetts on the other. There are about 4,000 men there now but a big transport came in last night and they are packing in about 700 men. I don't know when our turn will come (to depart). I hope soon, as it will soon be cold, we are in tents. Write soon as you receive this as I may go soon and I want to hear from you before I leave for the front. They say we are assigned to the 9th Maine but I don't know that for certain.

- - -

By the 15th of October he is in Virginia and writes from Chapin's Farm:[54]

- - -

Dear Mary:

- Oct. 15. We landed and marched about 6 miles to this place reaching it about sunset. It is only 8 miles from Richmond; only a picket line between us and the rebels, who are about a mile from us. There was a fight on this spot only the day before we got here, there is a rebel shell laying within ten feet of where I am writing, thrown there day before yesterday. There are three rebel forts within a mile of us. Our men attacked them but were repulsed. The 9th Maine (our regiment.) lost 40 killed and wounded, we met them going out in ambulances yesterday. The weather is very fine but the nights are very cold which makes it bad as we lay out in the open air and have no fire. They promise us our tents tomorrow. We are not yet organized so I don't know what Company I shall be in. My health is good, I have no chance to write much, sitting on the ground, with my knapsack for a writing desk but I wanted to give you the directions so that I

---

[54] Also spelled as Chaffin's.

could hear from home. Give my love to Mother and Abba; tell Flora I have seen lots of Negro babies.

- - -

Flora, his youngest daughter, was born 1858, and was only seven when David left for the war. She assuredly had many questions on his leaving and the noble fight to make all men, women, and babies free.

- - -

The 16th he writes:
- Worked on entrenchments, digging up the sacred soil of Virginia.

- - -

To contrast Libbey's life during the war, Eckstorm interleaved the following journal notes from the prior spring when he was in the Maine woods.

- - -

The spring previous he went on the drive as usual, and his journal of the drive is worth comparing with his war journal, for it is these notes of the woods which sings the battle-note. It is in his river-driving that we get the uplift of adventure and of danger. Even to those to whom the names mean nothing, there must be a thrill in the way the story of the drive of '64 plunges ahead. He was on the Mattawamkeag, and, — not to begin at the beginning: —

1864:
- May 25. Got over the upper pitch of Jimskiticook.
- May 26. Got onto the head of Scataract.

- May 27. Drove over Scataract.
- May 28. Big jam below; worked on Gordon Falls. Cleared Gordon Falls of middle jam.

- May 29. Worked on big jam below Slewgunda Island; got it all off.
- May 30. Drove over Ledge Falls; threw my ankle out of joint.
- May 31. Laid still.
- June 1. Drove over Slewgunda.
- June 2. Drove over Gordon Falls, leaving wings, 400,000.[55]
- June 10. Arrived home.[56]

To the stranger this list of rapids is but a roll of barbarous names; yet each one stands for a hundred dangers, a thousand difficulties, all overcome at last, and the great drive sweeping on victoriously down to the boom. Comparing this listing of going over falls in a boat, his record of time with the army is

---

[55] Likely referring to leaving wing jams and the amount of lumber.

[56] Jimskiticook is now Kingman, Maine. Slewgunda was a place of many bad jams. In July of 1846, the Twenty-Sixth Maine Legislature passed Chapter 357, stating, "No person shall draw or put into the Mattawamkeag River, or its tributary streams, for the purpose of being run through a place called Slewgunda any log, mast or spar or other timber, exceeding forty feet in length," with fines in the amount of twenty dollars per log assessed and forfeit of the logs. These were the drives of full-length trees, not pulp wood. The pitch at Slewgunda caused these logs to jam.

tame.[57] For war as the soldier sees it, is very often indistinguishable from ditching and toting, unless when varied by spells of no rations.

For David Libbey war was mostly lugging bags of oats out of vessels, — hundreds and thousands of bags of oats, the food of cavalry horses, — that, and heavy marching.

Though he made all the sacrifices, performed all the labors, endured all the hardships of war, and exhibited the qualities of a good soldier, David Libbey had no chance to distinguish himself. He was in battle but once and that was within two weeks of his arrival in Virginia. Stunned by the explosion of a shell, he "lay on the field all night in a steady rain, sick, dizzy, and faint." It was a month before he fully recovered; but with this exception he saw nothing of actual fighting.

That battle of most interest occurred late in October of 1864.

- - -

- Oct 31. Dear Mary,

I wrote you a line a day or two ago. I was so sick that I hardly knew what I wrote or when I did write and I dared not get any one to write for me, for fear of alarming you, but I expect my handwriting has done that. I am all right now, although my hand trembles badly yet and I walk like a drunken man on account of my head being dizzy. I will now give you an account of the fight. We were marched out of

---

[57] 'Tame' here is a matter of comparison. Surely, Libbey would have preferred his life in the woods, full of abundance, over the marching, sickness, and lack of rations he faced during the war.

camp Thursday at day light went through our breastworks a mile to the right (east) of our camp, then about two miles towards Richmond the last half a mile at a double quick; we came into a field where we found half a dozen regiments drawn up in two lines of battle, with a skirmish line in advance (a skirmish line is a line of men from three to twenty feet apart, a line of battle is two rows of men as thick as they can stand without crowding). Our brigade formed in line of battle behind the other two lines, we all laid down in this position, but the skirmish line which advanced and commenced firing on the rebels as soon as they reached the edge of the woods.

The second line of battle then took a position on the right of the first, and our line was ordered to take a position to the right of that, so as to form a single, long line of battle. Before we reached our position, the rebels had become fully aroused and opened on us with a battery through an opening on our right. We were ordered at once to lie down, while a battery on our left replied to them. The shot and shell flew over our heads both ways for fifteen minutes. When the rebel battery was silenced, we arose and moved towards our position which was close to the woods; in the edge of which was our line of skirmishes behind a breastworks they had driven the rebels out of. The air was full of flying bullets but only two men were hit before we got into position and were ordered to lie down close to the ground. We soon found this to be necessary for a lot of rebel sharpshooters had taken charge of us and a man couldn't stick his head up without having it used for a target.

To make things worse it began to rain and there we had to lay with our faces pressed to the earth from half past eight till five. I laid pretty still till about three when getting used to the bullets, I sat up and not wanting to make my clothes any wetter than they then were I got up and walked a few paces to the rear. While there two bullets went by my ears so near that they made them tingle. I went back and sat down facing to the rear. Just as I sat down a corporal in the rear rank (an old soldier) got up and put his pipe in his mouth. As he was going to light it, a bullet hissed over my head and struck him an inch back of the mouth, coming out under the opposite ear. The unfortunate man went down like a stone. I wasn't much afraid after that but sat up and watched our sharpshooters.

About five o'clock we were formed for a charge. Just as we got started a shell struck a few feet in front of me, bounded over my head and burst in the faces of a Pennsylvania regiment, ten paces in the rear, killing and wounding half a dozen men. The next instant a solid shot struck a white oak and glanced into our ranks ten feet to my right – killing three and knocking another ten feet without hurting him much.

We then received the order to charge; about a third of the regiment went in with a yell. The rest straggled along slowly and when about six rods into the woods began to fire. The situation we were in cannot be described. Why they did not kill all of us is a mystery, but they probably fired too high.

We advanced to the further side of the woods. Here we were met by grape, canister, shrapnel and musketry. A hell of fire! Over forty men fell in less time than it takes me to write it. It was here that the shell burst so near my head. I have no recollection of falling or getting up, but one of the men said I went down all in a heap. It seems to me that I went up and I shall always think so.

We fell back through the woods and laid on the field that night in a pouring rain. I didn't feel the effect of the shell much when I laid down and have no doubt the effect was aggravated by a cold. How I got back to camp that night I can hardly tell. I laid down every time the regiment stopped which was very often. The next day I was too sick to stand and wasn't much better the two next days. I am a great deal better today, better now than I was when I began this letter three hours ago. I shouldn't have troubled you with so many details but this is for all the boys in both families.[58] I meant to have said that the whole movement was made to keep the enemy in check while Grant attacked the south side railroad.

- - -

No letters or transcript entries are included until Thanksgiving.

- - -

- Nov 24. – Near Richmond, VA.,
                Dutch Gap along the James River.
Dear Mary,

If Thanksgiving Day is as cold, in proportion to the climate in Maine as it is in Virginia, I pity all of you. Our rainstorm cleared off, or rather, the clouds did, day before yesterday morning. It immediately began to grow cold, and night before last, the blankets froze over – my being all wet

---

[58] Referencing the Edgerly and Young families, along with Jim White.

by the long rain. Josiah was on picket and I slept alone, as our berths are made over each other to save room, two in each, and if one is gone his partner sleeps alone. I didn't sleep much, cold, but my turn came to go on picket yesterday and last night was colder than the one before. I was pretty cold, but was warm to what some of them were, you could hear men's teeth chatter for rods.

We had a very quiet time last night, but the night before I wrote Abba[59] we had quite a time. In the first place, two big guinea hens came into our lives; the boys gave chase to them but they escaped, they however captured a big black snake 4 ½ feet long, the first one I ever saw. About 9 o'clock in the midst of the darkness and rain, we were suddenly startled by the roar of musketry on our left. We rushed into our gopher holes expecting every moment to be attacked; but everything was quiet in our front, the heavy firing was over in an hour although there was more or less firing all night. The same thing was renewed the next night and the next.

We have since learned that the rebels attacked and carried our picket line close to Dutch Gap, capturing 125 men. The next night – we tried to take it back and failed, but succeeded in retaking in the next. About the time the firing stopped a deserter from the rebel picket line came in to our post, he was a very intelligent man, and was the best pleased person I ever saw when he found himself fairly inside our lines. He enlisted to serve the state of Virginia one year, and had been kept over three without being allowed to go home. He lives in Alexandria close to Washington.

---

[59] Abba was Libbey's youngest sister.

Today is perfectly clear and calm. We are going to have another cold night; the puddles were frozen hard enough to slide on this morning. I see by the papers that there has been any amount of stuff sent to the soldiers for a Thanksgiving dinner, none of it has arrived however, owing I presume to the shocking state of the roads occasioned by the late heavy rains.

I see by extracts from late rebel papers that they are expecting an attack from us in a very few days. Both here and on the other side the James River, they seem to be certain of it. I don't know but tis so, but don't see any signs of it. Some of the men have received gloves from home, the postage was only two cents – great care must be taken to put the wrapper on so that it won't slip off as in that case the gloves would be lost. The first edge of the wrapper might be pinned to the gloves and then lapped over and gummed, it needs to be drawn tight. I shall have to get you to send me a pair of mittens, my gloves won't last if I use them to cut wood in etc. They are nice to handle my gun in and ought not to be used for anything else; single mittens will do as well as any.

I received a letter from William Spearin today; he is well, and at Norfolk. I haven't received my *Courier* or *Transcripts*, I guess they are lost.[60] I got a pretty severe cold in the late rain storm. Aside from that I am well as usual. It is of no use for me to attempt to tell you how I want to see you and all the rest. If I had ten sheets of paper, each ten

---

[60] Referring to the Maine papers. *The Bangor Daily Whig and Courier* and the *Portland Transcript*.

times as large as this and should fill them all with nothing but that, you wouldn't have any better idea of it than you do now. I must leave it to your imagination.

We are to witness an awful ceremony tomorrow. A rebel spy taken in this regiment is to be shot, kneeling on his coffin, he was to be shot today but it was postponed on account of the day being one of National Thanksgiving. Three men from each company are detailed to shoot him; what must his feelings be today!

Give my love to mother and all the rest –write often.

Ever yours, D. S. L.

- - -

In such a letter, Libbey gives account of his days, no different from thousands of other soldiers. Yet, within these lines we see how he intended to convey the situation on the front, but also his health, how he missed his family, and instructions for sending parcels, the contents of which were all so dear to him to receive.

- - -

- Nov 25.

Dear Mary,

There has been a detail of fifty men out of our regiment sent to unload transports. Josiah and I are among them. It is five miles from the regiment, and we shall probably stay here two months. In that case I shall not be at my regiment the next pay day; and shall probably miss my pay. You will, therefore, have the kindness to send me five dollars. It costs a good deal for stationery, candles, etc. The Government provides some candles but not quarter enough and they cost 10 cents each at the sutlers; and I paid 25 cents per lb. for nails to build our winter quarters and everything else is the same proportion. Our work is regular from 7 to 5. We had the best chance to sleep I have had; bunk fitted up aboard a barge with plenty of straw to lay on.

Our letters will be sent to about every day from our regiment. It came down this morning, got my two Unions just before I started. The men have been here a week and we take the place of some that were sick and went back to their regiment.

Upon the whole I think it is better to be here as we get a good night's rest every night. I had roast turkey for supper. More than I could eat; have some left for breakfast.

Give my love to all. Good night, my dear Mary. I send you a hundred kisses and will bring you ten times more as many if I live to get home.

Ever yours, DSL

- - -

Image courtesy of the National Archives.

- - -

- Dec 3.

Dear Mary,

Since coming here I have written only once (to Lydia) with the exception of the few lines I wrote you the day I got here. The fact is I have had a severe fit of the blues and didn't feel like writing. They were brought on by derangement of the bowels and loss of appetite. For ten days I haven't tasted coffee or hard bread. It makes me sick to my stomach to think of them. I can eat a little bean soup generally about once a day. I took off my outer clothing to wash today and when I saw my bare arms, I was scared at first and then I laughed and laughed. I just wish you could see them! Upon my word they are no bigger than yours were when I came away.

You must not suppose there is any cause of alarm in all this. I am simply getting acclimated. I see daily plenty of men who have gone through the same process; men who went down from 180 lbs. to less than a hundred, most of them had the chronic diarrhea to contend with in the bargain. A man of good constitution is pretty sure to come out of it even when that sets in and without that there is no trouble at all. I have recovered my spirits for which I am thankful as I had rather be climate sick a week, than home sick one day.

A man got a box from home night before last and was generous enough to give me a piece of mince pie and a doughnut for which I was very thankful. When I wrote you for the $5.00, I forgot to tell you to send greenbacks, as state money won't pass here, but if you should happen to send it, I can get some of the officers to take it – and keep it until I get my pay, giving me a greenback for it. After getting my pay I can exchange back and send it home.

My missing *Transcripts* have come. I also received two more today. When you write again tell me how much buckwheat there was, also if there was any water run into the cellar, and how the potatoes save.

They wouldn't let me take my revolver away from Camp Berry and I left an order to have it sent back to Sunkhaze by express. If it hasn't got there please get someone to see Charley Haynes and see if he brought it up from Bangor or if it is down there. I don't want to lose it. It is getting dark and I must close as I have a few lines to write Walter about the rifle. Write often. Good Night

Ever yours, D. S. L.

Tell Flora I hope that Santa Claus will bring her something for Christmas. Love to all. Good Bye once more. DSL

- - -

SOLDIERS READING MAIL
Image courtesy of the National Archives.

- - -

In the prior letter we see a man, living on meager rations, losing his physical form, and he asks about water in his basement and what the crop of buckwheat yielded. From this we see, even though the men were in a fight for their lives, they lived on the news from home, waiting until the day they could return.

A good number of Libbey's letters show frustration with lost parcels and mail. During a time of civil war, and the postal routes being what they were, it is wonderful so many letters had been received and preserved as there were.

- - -

- Dec. 18.

Dear Mary,

I have received no letters since I got yours and Abba's containing the money a week ago yesterday. Thursday, I received my *Courier*, two *Unions* & two *Transcripts*. Friday, I received the mittens & gloves. Saturday, I received the three volumes of poems and last but not least your likeness which pleased me more than a letter.

I am happy to say that my health is a thousand times better than it was three days ago. I had what they call the intermittent chills & fever for five days. I would feel first rate in the morning, would eat a hearty breakfast of toast & tea and be able to do light work till noon when I would begin to feel distressed at my stomach and a severe headache which would grow worse till a burning fever set in which sent me to bed for an hour, when I would begin to grow cold, and have to sit over the stove another hour. This thing would last till about sunset leaving me to feel weak and dizzy till along into the night.

Yesterday, I felt decidedly better, eating some dinner and supper; the first time I had eaten more than once a day for ten days. Today I feel like a new man, am hungry all the time but don't want to overload my stomach.

I bought eight apples for twenty-five cents yesterday and stewed them. You had better believe it is nice on my buttered toast. It will last as much as four days.

We had baked beans for breakfast, and I ate my share. For dinner we have a nice soup of beef and potatoes. They say that our letters home are kept back on account of the expedition which left here ten days ago. Every regiment in our brigade went but ours. I should think that twenty thousand men went out of our corps and the 18th which lays side of it.

We all expected a big fight here, but as near as I can find out they went to Hilton Head to join Sherman. They all moved in the night and the greatest secrecy has been observed as it leaves us rather weak and the rebs might take advantage of it, but in my opinion, they are a great deal weaker than we are. If government has delayed our letters on that account, you will probably fret about me but I hope they went regular. Josiah Littlefield has been laid up with a lame back for the last few days but his health and appetite is good otherwise.

I saw Bagley's name in my paper among the list of paroled prisoners at Annapolis, he seems like one risen from the dead. I don't know when I have felt so glad as I did when I heard he was alive, poor fellow! I can imagine what he has suffered.

It has been summer weather here for the last week. The birds sing every morning. It rained a little today. Today being

Sunday we only worked a little over an hour this morning to finish unloading a vessel we couldn't get done last night. If we have enough ahead, we don't work Sundays, if not we do, as those 18,000 horses have to be fed every day.

Well, I wrote so far and laid it by to wait for the mail from the regiment. It has come and brings me a letter from you & Charley & Abba's Union & sugar.[61] The tea has not arrived yet. I thank Charley a thousand times for his interesting letter, will write him next, should have written before but knew that he heard my letters read. How glad I am he is going to be at home this winter.

Don't fret yourself because you didn't urge me more to get a substitute, I shouldn't have done it; and have never ceased to be glad that I didn't; grow more glad as each month goes by.[62] Next Wednesday makes a quarter of my time. I shall be glad when this letter relieves your anxiety on account of my health. Hope you will get my directions before you send the box. Good bye.

    Love to all. D.S.L.

- - -

There was no great variety or abundance in the commissary either.

For Christmas the record is: —

- - -

- Dec 25. Clubbed together and bought cabbage, which went nice for dinner.
- After the oats came the marching.

- - -

---

[61] His brother-in-law Charles Young. His sister sent him money.

[62] A reference to how some men paid others to go in their place to war as a substitute.

Eckstorm left a large gap in the transcription between the end of 1864 and February 1865. Additional journal notes found with the lost letters, appear to match exactly to some of the notes Eckstorm included; indicating she may have had these journal notes to review. A sample of the selections are included here. For dates not included, the reader should know, Libbey spent a good number of hours 'unloading sacks' of supplies.

- - -

WINTER QUARTERS
Image courtesy of the National Archives.

1865 - Jones Landing, James River, Virginia
- January 1. Snow & rain
- January 2. Worked all day took out 2121 sacks. Snow 2 in.
- January 8. Wrote Mary, began to unload a schooner, loaded with purveyors' goods.

- January 9. Finished unloading goods, confiscated two cans condensed milk and lots of cakes, others got cheese, raisins, etc.
- January 10. No work. Wrote Charley Stone. Received two books this A. M. from California. Letter from Abba
- January 13. Unloaded oats & hay in A.M.

- 15 Jan. 1865 – Jones Landing,

Dear Mary,

This is a beautiful Sabbath day. We had 1100 sacks of oats to take out this morning; there was some hay for the Darkies to take off, and we didn't get to work till nine o'clock, and as a good many of us wanted to write, we took them out "double quick," wasn't quite three hours. I went up to the regiment Friday afternoon and got back yesterday forenoon with my box. It was nine days in the orderly's tent at my company, close to the stove and I expected everything was spoiled. I didn't open it till I got it here and then I found everything in perfect order; just as nice as it was when you put it in. It seems as if the pies are better than they were when you baked them; at any rate they are the best ones I ever tasted. I never saw so much stuff in so small and compact a package.

What a good time I had unpacking it! I took up everything and looked at it thinking that your hands had touched it last (for it was not opened on the way). I was so busy and earnest that I never thought to eat a thing till I got everything out. That pail of butter is what I think the most of. I wouldn't take ten dollars for it today. If you had had a little square box, you could have saved your pail. It beats any box that has come to the squad. Some have had boxes as big again that didn't have as much in them.

You had to pay a pretty high express bill but they ask just about so much, without much regard to size. Some have got boxes not over half as big as mine that cost four dollars, and one man got one full as big again that only cost four fifty. I have put hinges on my cover so as to have it nice and handy. I couldn't get it all back into the box again but put the candles and dried apple into my bunk. I sleep alone as Josiah is cooking and has a hut on the bank where the cooking is done.

I sent Flora a little book presented by the Christian commission, tell her I got the stuff she put in my stocking and ate it before I did any of the rest. I got a letter from Abba on Thursday and answered it. Who sent the book in my box? It is bound exactly like the two I got from California. I have lots of reading now. I thank you and Sarah and all the rest a thousand times for all the nice things you sent me.

I have tasted both cakes; they are so nice I don't believe I shall have the heart to cut them, but keep them to look at.

You owe me a good many letters, pay up.

Ever yours, D.S.L.

- - -

- 16 Jan. 1865 – Jones Landing
Dear Mary,

I received letters from you and James tonight. I was astonished to see how many of my letters had failed to get home. I received Eliza Dudley's letter and answered it two days after. I also wrote Sarah a long letter after getting her last one, and have scolded to think that she didn't answer it.

I wrote one to James that he didn't get and I shouldn't wonder if there were some that you didn't get, for I have written either you or Abba every few days. You can judge how much I have written when I tell you that I have bought three quires of paper besides what the Christian & sanitary commission have given me and haven't over six sheets left; and by the way I shall have to call on you for some stamps. I am reduced down to seven. I am glad you got your order for some say we shan't be paid off till March, but you know what to do if you need money, raise it by a mortgage on the stock.

I got your box today and the nails and pegs all right. Also, the mittens and yarn. Tell Mother I haven't found my glove but don't need another, one is enough if I have to handle my gun which I don't expect to this winter. I don't think my letters are lost, only delayed. Be sure and write if Mrs. Dudley and Sarah have received theirs as I don't want to write them until I know; as I shan't know how to write.

Before you get this, you will have heard that there is a great talk of peace, over half the army think that fighting is over. I can't help thinking so myself, but don't allow myself to place any dependence on it. A few weeks will determine the question! Don't feel discouraged, the chances of my having to fight next summer are very faint. I will give you my reasons the next time I write. Good night. D.S.L.

Who sent me the quire of big paper? I filled one yesterday in a letter to California.

- - -

- January 20. Took out 2500 sacks; the best days work yet.
- January 22. Unloaded 1716 sacks.

- January 25. Worked. Rebel fleet started to come down the river from Richmond, one of them blown up. The other three blockaded under a high bank. Turned out under arms.
- Feb. 1. Pitched out shelter tents, received two books from California. Fine weather.
- Feb. 4. Came off guard. Sent poems home.
- Feb. 11. Steaming down the coast of N. C.
- Feb. 15. Marched all last night.

- - -

The 16th, 17th, 18th, 19th are repetitions of the same.
- 20th Varied by no rations; 21st half rations.

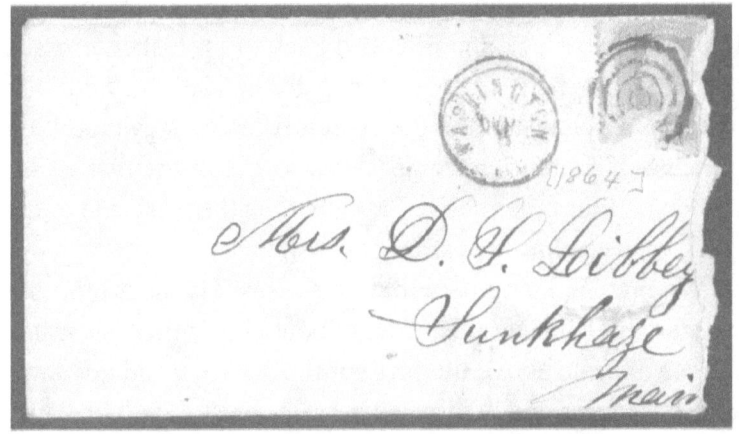

ENVELOPE FROM DAVID S. LIBBEY
Mrs. D. S. Libbey, Sunkhaze, Maine.
Sunkhaze, north of Old Town, was the postal address for Greenbush.

- - -

- Feb. 19. Marched nine miles, struck the road a mile in the rear of Ft. Anderson. Rebs escaped. Crossed the river and landed in rear of their work, rebs skedaddled.

- Feb. 20. Followed them to their second line, halted and threw up a breast work; no rations since last night.
- Feb. 21. Reconnoitered, got a half ration at noon.

- - -

On the whole there was a great deal more fun in running the wangun over Scataract and Slewgunda.[63]

- - -

- Feb. 21st, 1865, Front of Wilmington.
Dear Mary:

I suppose you have seen the letters I wrote Charley & Sarah, and so I will commence where I left off when I finished Sarah's letter. The next night after I wrote her, we fell in at 10 o'clock and marched back to Ft. Fisher, crossed the mouth of the river in steamers and landed in Smithville at sunrise. We rested there till noon when we again took up our line of march. Our object was to get in the rear of Ft. Anderson four miles above Ft. Fisher, on the west side of the river; a place almost as strong as Fisher.

We marched ten miles that afternoon. The next morning we started again and after going about eight miles we struck the road a mile above the fort but the Johnnys had got word of our coming and got by, two hours before we got there. They left in such a hurry that they never spiked their guns. We marched down to the fort, got aboard steamers at sunset, went four or five miles up the river and landed on the same side we were on in the first place, by this move we got in the

---

[63] Eckstorm's reference to rapids. The wangun, a spelling of wangan, is the supply boat, or supplies in general, for the river-driver crew.

rear of that swamp and line of works, I wrote Charley about. Of course, the rebs had to skedaddle out of that.

We landed at 2 o'clock at night. We were entirely out of rations. I had only half enough for supper. The next morning men offered ten cents apiece for hardtack, perhaps you never saw one; they are square, and about as big as a large cracker; ten of them is a day's ration. I got three of a man who had refused ten cents apiece for them, by letting him have a mess of tea and sugar. We started towards Wilmington about 10 o'clock, a brigade of colored troops in front. We drove the rebs all day, taking a few prisoners and having a few men wounded. About sunset we reached their outer line of works, four miles from the city. We worked till 10 o'clock, throwing up a breastwork and laid down tired and hungry.

This morning we were a savage set, none of us had tasted food for 24 hours and some not for 36. About 10 o'clock we got a half days ration of hardtack, coffee, sugar and fresh beef. Five hardtacks for men that hadn't eaten anything for almost two days! I could have eaten fifteen but only ate three, for I don't know when I shall get any more. We had not a speck of salt to put on our beef but I didn't mind that any. I got a piece of suet and fried mine in the fat of it and I never tasted anything sweeter. I carry a tin plate on purpose to fry in, putting on a split stick for a handle.

We are in plain sight of the rebel works. We were putting out our picket relief just as I was about to begin this letter. The officer in charge was foolish enough to march them out in a body. The rebs opened with a twelve pounder; one of the shells burst in their midst wounding a man from Company A, severely in the leg, and tearing another belonging to the 13th Infantry dreadfully; one of his arms was smashed at the elbow, the other at the wrist, and the flesh torn off his thigh. Some of the pieces flew whizzing over our heads. The men ran for the breastworks, but they only fired three shots.

We are strengthening our breastworks, what our next move will be I don't know, we shall probably see some hard fighting before we get the city. The news of the evacuation of Charleston was read to the men this morning. Regiment after regiment cheering as they heard it.

My health is perfectly good, the lack of food don't affect me any, I am used to it. I have "put in" five months today. Give my love to all.

Good Bye. D. S. L.

- - -

- Feb. 22. Rebs evacuated Wilmington. Marched into the city. Followed them out nine miles and captured 800.
- Feb. 23. In camp. Raided got pork, peanuts & turnips.

- - -

Then comes an episode with a dramatic spark in the heart of it: —
- Feb. 24. Detailed to cook for the Andersonville prisoners who are to be received into our lines here.
- Feb. 26. First squad of exchanged prisoners came in, all in a horrible condition, — lousy, filthy, and emaciated; fed them on hard-tack, coffee, and beef.
- Feb. 28. Prisoners come in at the rate of 1,500 a day.
- March 2. Saw Capt. George A. Manning.
- March 3. Mostly sick that came through today.

- March 4, All sick ones today; the victims of rebel cruelty and starvation; a heart-sickening sight. May the justice of God overtake their murderers!

- - -

In the original book for the entry of March 4, there is a disconnect in the letters found at Duke University for the same date.

The words in Libbey's hand are shown in this image and transcribed below:

- Sat. 4 - All sick ones today. The victims of rebel brutality and starvation. Exchange at this place, concluded came back to my regiment, which had moved back within two miles of Wilmington.

Why the difference between the two accounts?

Could there have been two sets of notes?

Were the words Eckstorm wrote in that section merged from a different section no longer with the Duke University file?

No conclusion can be made on the discrepancy with the information at hand.

Eckstorm continued from this section as follows:

Capt. George A. Manning, (who Libbey saw on March 2), was just out of Andersonville. Manning was a boyhood friend of David Libbey's.[64] Meeting among the released prisoners, surrounded by hundreds of others whose famished faces multiplied the horrors of the tale, they rehearsed the still more harrowing story of the brother, Capt. William C. Manning, just out of Libby Prison.[65] It is the thought of his friends' suffering which prompts the outburst of two days later, — the only vindictive utterance which I have seen anywhere in these journals.

Here follow a soldier's brief notes of the closing days of the war. From the 16th of March to the 14th of April, David Libbey's regiment was marching to join Sherman at Raleigh. They marched one hundred and eighty-five miles in thirteen days, aside from what he may have neglected to note. It was marching, laying corduroy roads, making pontoon bridges, taking them up again, and marching on, with the thunder of Sherman's artillery ahead, like the pillar of cloud which guided the Israelites.

---

[64] George A. Manning, (1836-1913), birthplace, Old Town, Maine. Manning was taken prisoner in February of 1864, and this date must have been his exchange date.

[65] Most likely, this refers to William C. Manning's time in a Confederate prison at Richmond, Virginia (Some records put his imprisonment at Salisbury, North Carolina.)

LIBBY PRISON

A Confederate Prison at Richmond, Virginia.
The name is coincidental. Prior to the infamous use as a
prison, the building was a ship's chandlery, a supply store for
ships and seamen, and a grocery business operated by a man
named Libby.
Image courtesy of the National Archives.

- - -

- March 16. Marched twenty miles. Threw away my woolen
blanket. Worked till midnight laying corduroy road in heavy
rain; then it cleared off cold.
- March 21. Time half out. Out of rations.
- March 22. Heavy fighting in front of us all night. Rebs got
whipped. Shot a pig.

- - -

- March 30th 1865, Magnolia, N. C.

Dear Mary,

I always feel glad when I have a chance to write you; for I know how anxious you are, and how thankful you must feel when you get a letter and know that I was well when I wrote; although you cannot tell where I am by the time you receive it. This time you can rest content, for we are in a place where we expect to stay all summer and a nice place it is; on high ground in the interior of the State and just as healthy as it is at home.

I wrote Abba yesterday, and while writing received a mail containing a letter and 4 books from Louis; a letter enclosing $5.00 from Mary (to buy candles with she said), also my *Courier* in which I found a list of the drafted men. Today I received a letter from you and one from Daniel, both containing a list so I think I am pretty well posted by this time. You wrote me that Daniel & Charles were going to try and get subs. I never was more astonished in my life; the rebellion is at its last gasp, with starvation staring them in the face at Richmond; with every rebel soldier driven out of South Carolina, and all of North Carolina except one corner; with Sherman's army victorious at all points, and only waiting for shoes and clothing to advance and crush the last remains of treason in the cotton states.

With all these facts I say looking one in the face, a laboring man must be crazy to pay seven, or five, or three hundred dollars for a substitute. If I was at home and knew as much about the desperate straits to which the Rebels are reduced as I do now, I would not pay one hundred or even fifty dollars, for a substitute, so help me heaven. All the people acknowledge themselves whipped, even the worst rebels say the same thing; three fourths of the army believe this thing will be ended before the 4th of July; and there is hardly one who believes that there will be another heavy battle. The rebels must come under, and the sooner the better for them, and they know it. I hope you will believe this and have too much good sense to grieve one minute because the boys are drafted, they can all leave very well, with the exception of Theodore; it is bad for him on account of his farm, and large family; he will lose the chance to put in a crop, but I have no doubt but he will be at home again before the snow comes.

I will now change the subject and write you what I have been doing since we left Wilmington, a fortnight ago yesterday. If you received my last letter, you will remember that I was detailed as carpenter the night before we started. I was ordered to report at Brigade headquarters in heavy marching order; and while over there the men's knapsacks in the regiment were all inspected by the Colonel. Every belonging was taken out but one shift of underclothing and either an overcoat or blanket – as they chose – but not both. They were also allowed to carry their shelter tents and rubber blankets, but these are always carried, after everything else is thrown away. As I was gone my knapsack was not inspected, so I didn't turn in anything as I did not know whether I was going with the regiment or not. However, I gave away my two pairs of stockings which I had worn almost six months. I also gave away part of my paper and envelopes as I had a quire and a half. Remembering how we lacked for food on our other march, I provided well for this one. I had about two quarts of rice in my knapsack and a big piece of pork, besides my regular rations in my haversack. They had detailed carpenters & bridge builders from every regiment in the division.

We were formed into three companies and when the division started, we marched in the rear. We started at noon the 15th and marched about nine miles that afternoon. The next morning, we started early. The day was very warm and about 10 o'clock the men began to suffer from the heat and to throw away clothing. Some of them threw away everything but their tents & rubber blanket, and for miles the road was strewed with overcoats, blankets, shirts, drawers and knapsacks. I don't know as ever I suffered any more with the heat in my life than I did that forenoon; I had on too many clothes, and the sweat run into my eyes and nearly blinded one. My head was dizzy and I could scarcely keep the ranks, but I managed to keep along till a halt was sounded to allow the men to rest. I took advantage of it to throw away my drawers; I then took off my blouse and put it in my knapsack and unbuttoned my vest and shirt bosom. My grub I was bound to stick to, if I threw away every rag of clothing I possessed. I had no trouble after that to keep up with the rest.

Just at night we came to a swamp where the water was up to the men's hips. All the troops crossed over, but our detail, which stayed back to fix the road so that the train could cross. Our train was five miles long and consisted of artillery, ammunition, ambulances and provision wagons. There was about a quarter of a mile of soft mud before reaching the water; this we had to corduroy, using fence rails for that purpose which luckily were plenty. It began to rain about dark and poured in perfect torrents 'til 11 o'clock when the wind got into the north and it cleared off cold. We finished the corduroy at 12 o'clock, it was too dark to lay the pontoons across the water. So thoroughly drenched and half chilled we left off work, and stood round fires till morning.

The next morning, we laid the pontoons and the train began to cross. It was a slow job. We had to wait till it was all across so as to take up the pontoons, about the middle of the afternoon. I found that they would not get across in time for us to take up the pontoons that night, so I took my gun and started off to find a pig. After going about a mile, I found a splendid one, which would weigh about a hundred. If I didn't eat a pile of fresh pork that night and the next morning, then nobody ever did.

We took up the pontoons early the next morning and marched about eleven miles and overtook the Division who had halted the day before at noon to wait for the train; they being out of rations. There we learned that Goldsboro was taken which altered all their plans, I suppose, for they dismissed the detail and I joined my company.

Our march for the next three days was through the most beautiful country I ever saw. Splendid houses approached by avenues shaded by lofty trees; great fields of winter wheat of a beautiful dark green, and half as high as your knees, and everywhere orchards of peach trees in full bloom whose fragrance filled the air and whose beauty charmed the eye. Very little damage was done as we passed through, nothing more than to "take up" all the bee hives and wring the necks of all the chickens, turkeys and geese that the boys could catch.

We had a swamp to wade every day, and sometimes two, but we always were allowed time to take off our stockings and roll up our pants so that it didn't hurt our marching any. We were far ahead of the train when we joined Sherman and most of the men got out of rations over a day before they came up, but my rice and another pig that I got the first day I got there gave me plenty to eat and also enough for my tent mates. We started back again after getting rested as Sherman didn't need us. The night before I got here, I shot another pig, the fattest thing I ever saw. He would weigh about 50 lbs. Josiah dressed him and put him in our knapsacks and brought him here, we have feasted on the nicest pork since then.

We also have got some corn meal and some sorghum syrup since we got here so you see we live like pigs in clover. Sorghum is better than our common molasses but not as good as sugar house syrup. It is very clear and is nice to eat on hasty pudding or with hardtack but it has a slight sour taste which I think must require it for cooking purposes.

This place is on the Wilmington and Weldon Railroad; about half way from Wilmington to Goldsborough; the distance between those two places is 85 miles by rail, but a hundred by the country roads. I was paid three months' pay yesterday and will send you some money as soon as I can do so safely. I dare not trust it by mail, but we shall soon have an express office opened here. We are not permanently located yet. Our campground is staked out just back of the church nearly half a mile from here; if it hadn't rained, we should have moved today; shall probably do so tomorrow.

My health is excellent; I weighed 163 lbs. today, very lightly clothed. I am happy to announce to you that I have entirely recovered my "lost manhood." As I expect to stay here some months, as this road is to be kept open, which cannot be done without a guard the whole length, as the guerillas would destroy it.

I believe I have never since our marriage told you, or wrote you anything that my sisters have said of you in their letters, but while up to Sherman's front I received two letters, one from Sarah the other from Emma, written in Maine and California, the two extremes of the Union. I read them within five minutes of each other and I cannot forbear copying what they each say of you. Emma writes: "She (Mother) has one of the most dutiful of daughters in Ann,[66] where could you find another who would put up with all Mother's foibles like her, she had been more kind to her than her own daughters; at least she had been more thoughtful." Sarah writes: "Ann is more of the best of wives, and so kind to Mother, if you had searched the world over you could not have found another one who would have got along with all of Mother's ways as she had done."

It may be some consolation to you while undergoing the hardships which are entailed upon you to know that your kindness and worth is appreciated.

I hope Flora got the ring I sent her from Wilmington. I paid for it today. I have thought a thousand times of her singular behavior when I came away, a person 20 years of age could not have been any more self-controlled than she was.[67] I couldn't help laughing when I read how she acted when the rest were drafted. I can see my own disposition

---

[66] Referring to her sister-in-law Mary Ann Young Libbey; likely used to differ between their sister Mary.

[67] Flora was six years of age when David Libbey left for the war.

there. J. Littlefield is my tentmate and if anything should happen to him, I should be sure to write. I write all his letters for him.[68] Love to all.

- Good night D.S.L.

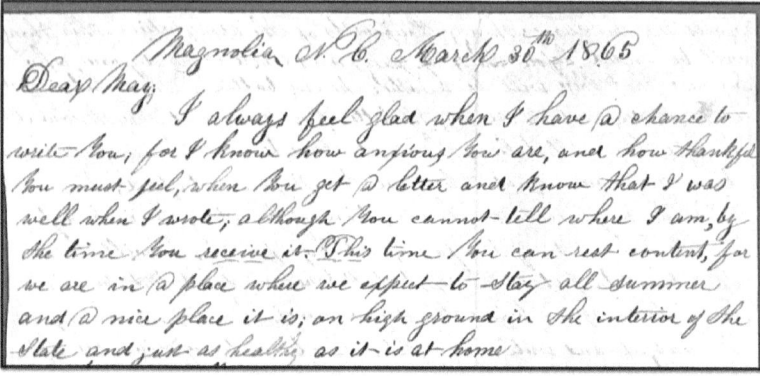

The start of the preceding letter. By this date, Libbey's writing is more care-free and it shows he is in better health and spirits. Even his penmanship has become less rushed and his letters are much more composed.

- - -

- April 5. On picket. 'Listened to the Mocking-bird.'
- April 6. News of the fall of Richmond.
- April 12. Heard of the surrender of Lee and all his army. Men cheered, drums beat, bands played; a great time all around.[69]

---

[68] Another reason these journal entries and letters from Libbey are unique is that many men didn't have the means to write. And we see here Libbey, who enjoyed his time corresponding with family and friends in Maine, and his sisters in California, had taken time to write for others.

[69] Lee surrendered April 9, 1865 at Appomattox Courthouse, Virginia.

- April 14. Joined Sherman and Schofield at Raleigh.
- April 16. Out of provisions; went foraging; shot a pig; got a canteen full of syrup and a piece of ham.

**PONTOON BRIDGE OVER THE
JAMES RIVER, VIRGINIA**
Image courtesy of the National Archives.

- - -

- April ?, 1865, Raleigh, N. C.
Dear Mary,

I suppose you have been a soldier's wife long enough to know that they are liable to move any minute. Therefore, this letter started over 80 miles from Magnolia, will occasion you no surprise to know that we were going to start when I sent you the letter enclosing twenty dollars a week ago Saturday but I thought it would save you some worrying if I didn't mention it. After Lee was routed out of Richmond an order came for all the troops to move. We left Magnolia early Sunday, marching so hard, about 30 miles farther to meet them.

The weather was awful warm and a number of men died on the route. The rebs had burned some bridges which delayed us some. We reached this place Friday night. Saturday morning it poured. We started in the morning and went about twenty rods when news came that Johnston was going to surrender his army. So we all went back. We didn't know what we went back for till we got in the campground when the Major rode along the line saying "no more marching boys, Johnston has surrendered his whole army." Such a throwing of hats and cheering you never heard. Our fighting is over, thank heaven. I can't tell you when we shall get home. It will take some time to get things straightened out but I hope to get home in time to do my haying. But I am so thankful to see the war closing that I don't think much about anything else at present. I sent you as I mentioned before, $20.00 the 8th of April. I hope you will receive it as you will need it to get the farming done.

My health is excellent. Tell Flora I will make her a bigger ring if nothing prevents when I get home. I can make just as good as one as Stevens. Give my love to all. I feel more glad on your Mother's account that the fighting is ended, than I do on my own.[70] You can now rest in peace. I owe lots of letters but have no means of answering them, and the capture of Lee and Johnston has so upset all my calculations that I don't know as I could write if I had everything to do with. I hope they will let Kennedy come home in time to do his farming.

Good bye for this time.

– Yours as ever, D.S.L.

---

[70] Now his brother-in-laws would not need to fight.

- - -

- April 18. News of Pres. Lincoln's assassination reached us this day.
- April 27. Funeral honors to President Lincoln. Thirteen guns in morning, one every thirty minutes till sunset, then thirty-six.
- April 20. Sherman's army started on its return.

- - -

Quite as thrilling as the broader views of commanders, the deeper studies of historians, are these brief personal records of the private soldier, who has no means of forecasting the next day's surprises. In ten lines of his journal he disposes of Lincoln, Lee, and Richmond — and shoots two pigs. The next day something else will turn up; but he is confident that, whatever happens, he is marching to the near close of the Great Rebellion.

- - -

- 7th May 1865, Raleigh, N. C.
Dear Mary,

I received letters from you and Abba a few moments ago; one written the 23rd – the other the 27th. Abba speaks of Sarah's getting a letter from me. I wrote it the day before I sent you the money and you should have received it when she did hers; but I don't think that you will lose it, it is probably delayed.

I also learned of the disastrous fire at Oldtown, from my *Courier*. I have no doubt but it was set by some devilish copperhead, Hilliard, Burgess and Blanchard being the strongest men in town.[71]

An image from the start of the preceding letter. The upside-down words are the final sentences at the conclusion of the transcribed letter.

- - -

Abba writes that she thinks that I don't get all the letters that you write as they had mentioned several times about my poems having come and I still kept asking about them. I think that I get all your letters but it takes some time to get one and get an answer back. I received your notices that the poems

---

[71] The term Copperheads, were applied to a faction of Democrats in the Union who opposed the American Civil War. These, Peace Democrats, as they were also called, wanted an immediate peace settlement with the Confederates.

arrived safe. But not till after I had enquired about them several times.

O, Mary! (don't laugh til you read the whole) I wish I could send you some roses. Such glorious ones you never dreamed of, thousands and thousands of them – acres and acres, I might say; and such roses; damask roses, as big and as bright as peonies; pale yellow roses, as big as your two hands; and bright golden yellow roses not much bigger than marigolds; China roses, and climbing roses, and tea roses, and moss roses, roses everywhere, the very air is heavy with their perfume. This is a beautiful country every way, with swelling hills and level valleys; with splendid mansions embowered in noble trees and all that nature and art can do is seen here in perfection.

We are encamped in a lovely grove on the side of a hill, about half a mile from the city. On the top of the hill just back of our camp is one of those fine mansions which the wealthy planters build for a summer residence. The carriage road comes up straight to within fifty rods of the house, and then sweeps up to the house in a half-circle on the other forming a circle nearly half a mile around it. This circle is not fenced but is planted with roses throughout almost its entire circumference.

The piece of ground enclosed by this circle is a beautiful green, full of noble trees. The house itself is in a perfect wilderness of flowers, shrubs and trees – but it no use – I might describe and describe, and then not convey to your mind a just conception of this most beautiful city with its lovely environs. Not the least of its attractions is the incomparable mocking bird which abounds in the trees all around and through the city – and who's wonderful power of song hold me motionless and almost breathless, sometimes for nearly half an hour.

I think upon the whole that I shan't go back into Maine again but will take one of the beautiful white slave girls which one sees here every day and settle down.[72]

I was safeguard in one of the rich citizen's houses for ten days but they, the guards, were taken off last Monday, and the streets are patrolled now night and day by soldiers who are detailed every 24 hours from the different regiments in our Brigade.

I was glad enough to get the stamps Abba sent me. I have had none but what I have begged or borrowed, for the last month. I have six books which I want to send home but cannot for want of stamps. If we should move, I should be obliged to throw them away as I have no means of carrying them, some thief having stolen my knapsack with everything I had in it: overcoat, rubber blanket, shelter tent, drawers, shirts and stockings. And what I valued more than all the rest, all my letters, along with Louis's likeness, there were over fifty – and I had carried them safely through all our long and tedious marches. Thank heaven they didn't get your miniature. I carry that over my heart (and the dear original in it) I should certainly have cried with sorrow and vexation had they got that to gaze at and make obscene sport over, after I have carried it so long and kissed it so many, many times. Please heaven I shall never part with it while I live. I also

---

[72] A section of this letter, where Libbey gives Mary a description of the flowers, was printed in the magazine, *FLORA – A Newsletter for the Friends of Duke Gardens* (Spring 1995). Is it not synchronicity that Libbey's eldest daughter was named, Flora?

saved my toilet case, containing my pens, stationery, thread, needles, etc. that being inside the house (they stole the knapsack off the porch table, while I was eating supper).

Give my love to Mother, Abba & dear little Flora. Don't look for me till September and rest satisfied that I am better off than I should be driving. My health is excellent.

The weather is very warm. Apples & peaches are half grown. I had some strawberries & cream – Mary dear; strawberries bigger than tame cherries.

Good Bye. Ever Yours, D.S.L.

- - -

The Header of the *Flora* Newsletter. The publication is no longer under this name.

- - -

In this prior letter, we read a change in Libbey's disposition. His mind on returning home, he has returned to his love of nature and his observation of the outdoors.

- - -

- May 23rd 1865, Raleigh N.C.

Dear Mary,

I have been waiting sometime to hear from home again before I wrote but by some reason my mail doesn't come. The Sisters in California had not heard from me since I landed at Fort Fisher. That was the first of Feb., and Mary's last letter was dated the 13th Apr. I wrote them in less than a week after I landed, and have written regularly since, but some cause delayed them and also their letters from home or else the folks at home neglected to write. I don't know when I have felt so bad as I did when I read Mary's letter and realized what their feelings must be, writing and sending me books, uncertain whether I was living or dead. She said all they could do was to hope for the best. They didn't know but that I had gone back to Virginia and was in the battles around Richmond. I am very sorry to have any one suffer anxiety on my account, but hope that they have heard from me long before this. You worry if you don't hear from me every week; I don't know what you would do if you shouldn't hear from me for two months. I am thankful that you have never been subjected to the trial, and hope you never will be. I expect you worry some as it is, but you have no reason to now that fighting is over and my health is so good. I am heavier than I ever was in my life before, weighing 165 lbs. with hardly any clothing on. I have weighed that once or twice before, in heavy winter clothing which, if I had on now, would make me over run 170.

News came to the regiment last week that all the men whose time expired before the 1st of Oct. were to be sent home at once, but we have learned that Granger, who is in command of the Brigade and also post commander, wants us to stop; for we are the best drilled, best dressed and best looking regiment there is in the division and there are over 200 men which would go out under that order, which would spoil the looks of the regiment. So they say that Granger is going to keep us as long as possible and as he is a man of considerable influence. He can keep us here till fall by representing to the war department that we are needed here. However as long as my health is good, I shan't grumble, although I should like to get home in season to cut my hay, but am thankful that I haven't got to march and fight all summer keeping my folks in a fever of excitement all the time.

I have got a new knapsack and under-clothing. They gave me a splendid new comforter with as much as ten yards of calico in it when I left Dr. Johnson's. When the blankets that were left at Wilmington got to the company, I stepped up and took one, as nobody knew but I had one in the box, there being lots of spare ones belonging to men who had gone to hospitals and would go from there to home, or – as is too often the case – to the grave. As I didn't need them both I got a box and Josi, Willard and I filled it with the comforter, blankets, spare clothing and the six books I had sent me and sent it yesterday by express to Oldtown as we are the only ones that know how to divide the stuff it will have to remain there till we get home, but it would be well enough to get someone to look after it and see that it is stored in a dry place.

Tell Flora I have tried to get some pretty white boys to go home with me to be her brother but they won't go. I can get lots of black ones though and will bring one if she wants one. Give my love to Mother; tell Abba I am waiting to hear where Charles is before writing her. Tell Isaac's wife I expect to get married again myself when I get home, and consequently shall have wedding cake enough of my own. Love to all. Good bye.

Yours ever, D.S.L.

- June 1st/65, Raleigh, N.C.

Dear Mary,

Yours of the 23rd I received in less than two hours after writing to Abba. It contained the best news I ever received in my life. I had dwelt so much on what Bing[73] wrote, that I had become firmly convinced that Mother would not recover. I trembled so that I could hardly stand, when I took hold of the letter and saw Abba's well-known hand writing on the back. I went into my tent and tried to regain some portion of my natural firmness, but to no purpose. I held the letter in my hand unable to master sufficient courage to tear it open. At last, I thought that perhaps it was no later than Bing's and had been delayed (Steve don't post mark half his letters). So, I tore it open with trembling fingers. I believe my eyes took in the date and half the page at a single glance. The next instant they were filled with tears of joy and thankfulness. I cannot write you any news which will give you as much pleasure as yours did me, still I flatter myself.

The news I am about to write you not be unpleasant. We are going home immediately. Of that there is not the shadow of a doubt. Orders have come to the regiment to muster us out at once. They are making out the muster-out rolls and descriptive lists. An inventory has been taken of our guns, equipment, etc., preparatory to turning them in to our respective Captains; all drilling has ceased, and we are going home, no mistake. Of course, I can't tell you when we shall start, it may be in 24 hours and it may be a week, but if

---

[73] Bingham Edgerley, cousin by marriage.

nothing in Providence prevents, I shall be at home in season to celebrate the coming 4th of July.

I send Flora rose leaves. Tell her to lay up a good pile of kisses for me. It is not necessary to give you any notice of that description, as I presume you are already provided with sufficient quantity. This is my last sheet of paper; plenty of oil lamps left. Sent all the books home in a box.

Your money was undoubtedly stolen as Crocker's wife got hers which went in the same mail. It is just as well however, as though I had kept it; for I have had my wallet stolen and they would have got it all as it was, they only got one dollar.

Good bye,

Ever yours, D.S.L.

- - -

- June 7th, 1865. Raleigh, N.C.

Dear Mary,

I suppose if you don't hear from me you will think that I am on my way home and so will begin to look for me about a fortnight too soon. As near as I can find out we shall be mustered out Saturday and start Monday. We are going by the way of Gaston and Petersburg, but I don't know whether we will go from Petersburg to Richmond and from there to Washington, or go to city point and take a transport down the James to Fort Monroe and up Chesapeake Bay and the Potomac. If we start Monday morning, we shall reach Gaston (by rail) that night. We will have to March from there to Petersburg – 80 miles. That will take five days so we shall get there about the 17th. Allowing eight days to get from there to Portland that will be the 25th. Give them five days to finally discharge and pay us off. That will be the 30th so I should still have ample time to get home the 4th.

I have stated the shortest time in which you are to look for me. We may be delayed a week in Washington for a review or something else, or we may not start so soon as I have stated, but if you don't receive another letter in a week after getting this you may think we have started, as I shall write more if we don't start before a week from Sunday next. I received a letter from (*name illegible*) with lots of stamps, have sent all the books to Oldtown by express, sometime ago.

I wish you were here to go cherrying, or berrying, or pluming with me. Plums like those Fothergill raises, only better, grow wild here. They are just getting ripe; cherries are almost gone. A fruit they call dewberries is also ripe. They look just like our running blackberries only they are as big as my thumb and melt in your mouth, but best of all are the mulberries which grow on trees two feet through they are black, about as big round as a blackberry but twice as long and all the way of a bigness, looking some the shape of a caterpillar. They don't taste like a blackberry, strawberry or raspberry but remind you of all three, when you are eating them. There are no raspberries here I think; strawberries are gone and blackberries most ripe.

Give my love to Mother and all the rest. Be patient and don't fret if I am detained a week.

Good bye,
Ever yours, D.S.L.

The start of the prior letter from June 1.
This letter is typical, in which the shortage of paper requires
Libbey to append the end of his thoughts back to the
beginning of the first page. He often writes in the margins and
upside down to fit as many words as possible on his limited
paper supply.

- - -

The Final Letter

June 18, 1865 Raleigh, N.C.

Dear Mary:

I wrote Sarah that if we did not start before today, I would write. Well, we have not started, so I proceed to fulfill my promise. I can tell you in one minute how the case stands so that you will know just as well as any of us does when we shall start.

There were fourteen regiments in this division. They began to muster them out a fortnight ago today, and have mustered out seven. At that rate it will take another fortnight to muster out the other seven. When our turn will come, no one in the regiment knows, so you now know just as well as any of us when we shall start.

I laughed when I read your complaints about having to live so much without a husband. I suppose you actually thought that you live without a husband, a great deal more than _I_ do without a _wife_. But if you had not only your husband, but your child taken away from you, I expect you would think it harder still.

As for my leaving you to go hunting, I only hope that I shall be able to. At present, I cannot come up the hill from the cook's tent to mine in anything like a hurry without being perfectly breathless when I get there. And I have nearly fainted away marching from the parade ground to the Company Street at a double quick, about ten rods, and yet my health is perfectly good, but I have no strength and no wind.

We have nothing to eat, the rations are about all played out. The government didn't expect it would take two months to muster out a few thousand troops and so did not furnish rations enough for so many men. At any rate, the rations are so poor that the surgeon has forbidden the officers to drill the men. And even the camp guard are not required to walk their beat, but are allowed to sit down in the shade.

From four to ten men die every day at the division hospital. I have seen so much of death since I came into the army that it will almost seem like coming from the dead if I live to get home, and my feelings if I am spared to see that blessed spot once more can but be faintly imagined by those at home who know nothing of the horrors a man passes through in even a single campaign.

Three fourths of the deaths at present are the result of the men's own carelessness. Some of them get too lazy and filthy to live, and others when they don't feel well lay right down in their hot tents, day after day, which would kill anybody.

I go away, out in the country, every day almost. The heat about melts me coming back, but it is a great deal better than laying in camp all day. Half my living is on plums and berries. Blackberries are ripe and plentiful. I picked two quarts in a few moments today, about a mile and a half from camp.

Since I began writing, a report has come into camp that we are to be the last regiment mustered. I have no reason to doubt it and don't expect to get home before the 20th of July.

Keep up a brave heart, as I have to do. I also have to encourage others which you are not required to do, for Crocker has been very slim for a fortnight and I have to keep him from losing courage, else he would die as sure as fate if he did; a man's doom is sealed if he loses heart here.

Give my love to all. I am in hopes to see you a "happy woman."

Ever yours,
D.S.L.

- - -

In that final letter David Libbey tells Mary how he is fairing. Imagine, being so close to going home, yet near starvation because the country you served has neglected to provide for the army. In the letter he answers her questions about hunting. She must have asked him his plans for returning to the woods he loved so much. How it must have pained him to know his strength was so meager he wouldn't be able to follow a deer, let alone drag one out of the woods.

Based on his account of this final letter from the war, Eckstorm must have been aware of Libbey's poor condition. In the next paragraph she reports on his ailments and how the war affected him. Fortunately, he regained his strength. he would return to digging knees and accomplishing so much more in his days yet to come. Not only would he leave Mary to go hunting, but he would depart for a much longer time than the ten months he spent away during the war.

- - -

On the 29th of June, David Libbey was mustered out. On the 11th of July he is home again. He is not so well as when he went away. Fever, jaundice, malnutrition, and sciatica have done their work, and the last was to stay with him all his life.

For nineteen springs he had slept two months at least in every spring on the cold, wet ground, often with no covering from the rain; all his life he had worked out of doors in all weathers and exposure and it had done him no harm; but in nine months of army life he is half broken down by the hardship.

It is facts like these which open our eyes to realize what was demanded of men during that last year of the war. But now Johnny comes marching home, and once more he plunges into the life he loves, — trout-fishing, partridge-hunting, bee-hunting, going on an occasional "side-hunt" for sport, or to a "piling-bee" at some neighbor's.[74]

Sometimes there was a dance.

CANOE BY THE SHORE
Libbey once again enjoyed the Maine woods.
(Editor's Collection)

---

[74] Piling-bee was maybe another terms for a 'logging bee,' a gathering where neighbors helped neighbors clear land of timber.

A CARRYING PLACE
(Editor's Collection)

DOWN IN MAINE

It seems to me
 The sun shines brighter,
It seems to me
 The snow is whiter
It seems to me
 That care grows lighter
     Down in Maine

It seems to me
 The water's purer,
It seems to me
 The clouds are fewer,
It seems to me
 All life is truer
     Down in Maine.

It seems to me
 The sky is clearer,
It seems to me
 That friends are dearer,
It seems to me
 That Heaven's nearer
     Down in Maine

Author unknown.
The poem appeared in The Northern, September 1921.

LUMBER CREW AND COOK ROOM

A lumber crew with the cooks.

Taken near South Basin, Mt. Katahdin.

(From, *The Northern,* 1922.)

HOME AGAIN

ONCE back home in Maine, Libbey resumes his pioneer lifestyle. He spends time with friends, and is also back in the woods hunting, to earn money, to feed his family, and simply to enjoy the Maine woods again.

The wholesome woodland life has renewed its charm, and it is good to see with what zest he follows it. Here is his record for a few days at bee-hunting: —

- Sept. 12. Got 22 pounds honey.
- Sept. 14. Got 75 pounds; lost 25 pounds.
- Sept. 17. Got 50 pounds.
- Sept. 22. Got 47 pounds.

In ten days he got over 200 pounds of honey besides what was lost, — splendid winter store of sweets at a time when sugar was too dear to buy.

- Oct. 17. Had a dance! Pratt played same tune for twelve hours!!

One wonders what that tune was!

But here is a record like the tolling of a bell in the forest:

- 1867, June 7. Tried to find Sister Almira's grave, who was buried at Edinburg thirty-one years ago; unable to find it.

She was the next older than David, only a child of eleven when the summons came, and somewhere under the forest by the great river she sleeps apart from all her kin. Not men alone are buried in the forest to be forgotten, women and little children lie there also.

- - -

With the next few journal entries Eckstorm chooses passages from differing years that relate to Libbey's times in the woods.

- - -

From his journal one gets little notion of the dangers and hardships involved in the woodsman's life, as David Libbey led it. He always understates his peril or endurance. Neither of the following, for example, sounds like a hair-breadth escape: —

- 1872, Dec. 22. Tremendous wind; snow nearly suffocated us before we got through the fields; two feet of snow in the woods; sunk to our knees at every step, — on snowshoes, too! Took us five and a half hours to get to Work's Mills, seven miles.

- 1858, Feb. 10. Got lost on Military Road; crossed it and did not know it; kept on going west to Carleton Brook (very

cold and windy), on to Maddaceunk Lake;[75] down the lake
to an old camp; found a spread and stayed there till sunrise;
then went down to Thibadeau's camp, got something to
eat, and came back to camp.

Interpreted, this record reveals such dogged endurance as
few men can equal. I have the story in full from his son and
also from his hunting companion, James White. In a strange
country, expecting to get his bearings by the old Military
Road to Houlton,[76] Libbey crossed the unbroken woods road
without seeing it in the twilight and was lost. His wet
clothing froze quickly in the cold night wind, and his
matches would not light. None of the ordinary expedients of
the bewildered woodsman could save him; he must have
shelter and fire or perish, and he was alone, after dark, in an
unknown country. Twice his life was saved by the merest
chance happening.

When nearly exhausted, he sat down on a log to rest a
moment and fell asleep; but for his rifle rolling from his
knees and striking on his feet, he would have frozen to death
sitting there. He rose and stumbled on, coming in time to a
camp. But the camp was deserted; no food, no fire, his own
matches useless. He sat down on the edge of a bunk, resigned
to a fate which was not far off, when, falling backward from

---

[75] Now spelled, Mattaseunk Lake, located east of Medway,
Maine.

[76] Today Route 2A that runs from Macwahoc 45 miles to
Houlton. In a day when roads were few in this part of Maine, it
is interesting that this is the marker one is given as a point of
reference.

exhaustion, he struck upon an old spread left by the crew, and had just enough consciousness left to roll himself over and over until it was closely wrapped about him. That spread saved his life, for it held in the natural heat of his body and thawed the ice from his clothing.

In the morning, when he crept into Thibadeau's camp, he was too used up to drink the hot coffee the cook poured for him. Finer almost than his courage in facing danger is such a dauntless struggle against fate; but with the trained woodsman this resistance to death is almost automatic, and many of them have saved their lives by refusing to die when death looked inevitable.

At times, however, the danger was sharp but brief: —

- 1867, May 11. Worked on rolling dam just above Ham's on the Mattawamkeag till eight o'clock;[77] got knocked in by a log striking my cant-dog; went over dam and was carried to bottom at foot of apron, severely bruising left leg, arm, and side on ledges. Swam over pitch under bridge and came out below. Ran wangun to chopping below Ham's.

One would suppose that a man who had been tumbled over a rolling-dam ten feet high and smashed upon rough ledges among a ruck of plunging logs, would have taken a day off instead of hobbling back to run the wangun-boats; for if there is any work on the drive which requires a whole man,

---

[77] A roll dam, or 'rolling dam,' is a dam without gates, built at the head of falls or rough water. It cannot retain any head of water, like a dam with gates, but by increasing the depth of water above the falls and presenting a smooth lip to the current, keeps the logs from stranding at the head of a pitch.

it is running those heavy boats, loaded with the provisions and outfit of the drive.

Three days after he notes down:

- S. Ruggles drowned while marking prizes a short distance below the bridge.

But three days before S. Ruggles would not have swapped chances with him.

After 1870 David Libbey was extensively engaged in getting out ship-timber. Few know that the ship is really built in the woods; that her frame is not chosen from a heap of timbers piled up at random, but that every timber is cut by specification and dressed to fit one of a series of patterns, called moulds, which the explorer carries with him into the woods.

"Moulding ship-timber" is shaping it after these patterns. The loss of even one of the smaller pieces might cause much trouble in the shipyard; therefore, the explorer works by contract. This explains the situation in the following extracts from the journal of 1871, when a sudden "breaking-up" in the spring threatened to leave Libbey with a ship-frame partly in the woods, where horses could not penetrate after the frost was out of the ground. This is a record of sheer grit, and for a small, light man an almost herculean labor. To appreciate it one must remember that this timber lay across two brooks which had risen under sudden freshet, flooding the low land between.

- 1871, April 12. Got navel timber and second futtock which Josi' had moulded. Got Littlefield and Flanders to yard the balance of Bunker Pond timber; couldn't get to it.[78] Tried to get to other; couldn't. Bridged the first brook; put on all hands and shoveled snow out of the road.

- April 13. Further brook flowed from one to two and a half feet deep in road for thirty rods. Littlefield twitched timber across it with his horses. All hands worked in water nearly to our hips.

- April 14. Littlefield began to twitch timber in the morning. Horses so chilled that he had to give it up. Offered him fifteen dollars to twitch till night; tried a few pieces and had to give it up. Tried to haul it across by hand after yarding it onto main road with a rope; too hard.

- April 15. Pulled the twenty pieces of timber out of the water and got five across in the a. m. King and Marble got fifteen across. Bridged a lot more on first brook, then helped the boys wade across balance of timber, six pieces. Flanders and Marble hauled it all up, forty-five pieces. Road all but impassable at first brook.
- April 16. Yarded the timber on Bunker Pond. Hand-sledded the last navel across first brook, three fourths of a mile, a big job. All the timber yarded, ninety-two pieces.

---

[78] To 'yard timber' is to get the timbers to a log yard, from where it could be floated down the river in a drive.

But the next day he finds twelve more pieces in Morton's Swamp and hand-sleds them out to the pond, where they were left on the ice in order to float free for driving when the ice broke up.

It is impossible for anyone unused to the rigors of a northern climate to imagine what it means to stand the most of five days, often up to the hips, in water so cold that horses are chilled half to death by it. Add to this that the man is a victim of chronic sciatica, and see whether the fighting principle is in him.

But the weather changes: —

-1871, July 14. Hottest yet!! Sided three navels, one taking us about all day. Seventeen boils on my back and hip. George Piper lost one day, boil on his leg!

- July 15. Sided four navels. Fell rock maple for keel. Geo. Piper lost one day.

- July 16. Finished keel piece number 7, rock maple, 47 feet. Sided two navels. Fell another rock maple for keel — a beauty.

- July 17. Finished keel piece number 8, 57 ft. long, the handsomest hardwood stick of timber I ever saw. Sided one floor, four navels.

- - -

In these entries, we seen an indication of the custom work being done. Each timber piece being sought is numbered for a specific purpose. These were not small pieces of wood by any means, as indicated for piece No. 8. For Libbey to remark on the beauty of this piece of timber amongst what were brief notations is saying something of the pride he had in his work

- - -

Thus, the work goes on, hot or cold, wet or dry, well or ill. Too often accidents interrupt it painfully. It is surprising to note the number of serious injuries received in this work. They occur often, though little note is taken of them. Here is an example: —

- 1871, Aug. 6. Began to dress knees; ax caught in a limb on the first knee and came down on left foot, cutting off end of little toe and splitting next one in two pieces and my foot in for over an inch. Dr. D---- dressed it; paid him $1.50.

- Aug. 13. Soaked off all the adhesive plaster from my foot to see what made it smell so offensive and found that the fool of a doctor had bound the piece cut off my little toe to the under side of the next toe! Got it off and washed it clean.

But there was to be a great function in Bangor, the opening of the eastern end of the first great transcontinental railway, known for many years by the high-sounding title of "European and North American" — as if, as Mark Twain said of Tasmania, the popular notion was that 'you got to it on a bridge.' So David Libbey, in spite of his cut foot, attended.

- Oct. 16, 1871. Took train for Bangor. Saw Pres. Grant and children, Nellie, Ulysses and Jesse, Gov. Perham, Sen. Hamlin, Gen. Babcock, Speaker Blaine and others at the Exchange Hotel.[79]

It was in November of this same year that David Libbey removed to Newport, Maine.[80] Here he spent the remainder of his life, happily placed, having for his near neighbors his two sisters, Abba and Lydia, who had married his old friends, Charles Young and James White.

- - -

In the year 1871, Flora was 13 years of age, Alice was five, and son Charles was three.

---

[79] The editor has corrected the record from the original text which listed the date as *August 16*. President Grant arrived by train to Bangor on October 17, 1871 for the official opening of the European and North American Railway. The President's train was comprised of seven cars of dignitaries and guards. Attesting to Bangor's prominence in the lumber industry, over 700 lumbermen and river-drivers took part in the parade.

[80] The Libbey family may have moved to Newport, Maine in 1870 or 1871.

A tree being prepared for digging out the 'knee.'
Image courtesy of *Josh Swan* –
J. W. Swan & Sons – Boats, Timber, Workshops

FROM MAINE TO SAN FRANCISCO

Eckstorm's next transcriptions from Libbey's journal are from the Centennial Year of 1876; a momentous year for David Libbey. To pay for his trip to the exposition in Philadelphia, he employed his nephews to dig knees with him in the Adirondacks. The digging was on land he had purchased the rights to a lot of timber ten years prior.

After attending the Centennial, he traveled to California to visit his sisters. There he would find work and spend a good deal of his leisure time writing essays for magazines and newspapers.

- - - - -

THE first time David Libbey ever travelled for pleasure was when he went to the Centennial Exposition.[81] Even then he paid his own way by forethought. Ten years before (1866), while hunting in the Adirondacks, he discovered good hackmatack, and now he arranged to have his nephews, Louis and Walter White, meet him there and dig knees. For three months they worked upon tracts where he had bought stumpage, and sent home several carloads of knees, worth much more in Maine shipyards than in New York.

---

[81] The Centennial Exposition of 1876 was held in Philadelphia, Pennsylvania. As a further note of interest, Manly Hardy also attended the exposition that year. It was on Hardy's return voyage he met with the Bangor Tigers following their river drive down the Connecticut River. That story is relayed in, *The Penobscot Man – Life and Death on a Maine River*, 2022.

While still in the Adirondacks his brother-in-law invited him to come to San Francisco for three years. It was a momentous decision for a man with a wife and three children; but the prospect was alluring, the love of travel was in him, and after only a month at home back he started, bound for the Golden Gate.

The 18th of November he got his first sight of the Pacific; the 20th he entered the employ of J. G. Hodge & Co., wholesale stationers, as receiving clerk. Who would guess now that the clerk who "spent the day checking fine stationery" was a moose-hunter from Maine; that a veteran bear-hunter "marked prices on goods and stacked them on the counter;" or an expert river-driver, for fifteen years head-boatman on some of the roughest water man ever put a boat over, was employed in "arranging Colgate's perfumery alphabetically in a closet?" It is the irony of life that takes this master of the manliest trades, who has braved winter's cold, laughed at the fiery fierceness of a northern summer's sun, and slept hundreds of nights upon the cold, wet ground with little shelter or none at all, and puts him at work hardly too heavy for a woman, and that under shelter, and in sunny California.

But San Francisco is a great opportunity for David Libbey. He sees much and enjoys much. For the first time in his life he hears good music and sees good acting. Never again did he have such an opportunity, and his journal shows that he improved it. He goes to Woodward's Gardens often; to the Tivoli Gardens twice; twice to hear the Vienna Ladies' Orchestra; to see Sothern as Dundreary, and Neilson, first as Juliet, again as Viola, then as Imogen in "Cymbeline" and as Isabel in "Measure for Measure," once a week indulging himself in some such treat, though he was a man sparing of spending upon himself, and his pay was not large.

He goes to the Opera Bouffe and to the "Black Crook;" but he also hears Stebbins lecture twice on Mohammed — "very good;" and the Old Folks' Concert — which is "splendid;" and he sees Denman Thompson in "Joshua Whitcomb," which he declares is "the best impersonation of Yankee character I ever saw."[82]

He sees Mojeska play Ophelia to McCulloch's Hamlet, and Rose Eytinge in "That Lass of Lowrie's." He hears Kellogg and Annie Louise Cary in "Aida," and then to "Mignon" when Kellogg, Cary, and De Murska sing together. He goes to the library to study Dore's illustrations of Dante's "Inferno," which he pronounces *powerful but fearful.*"

Much else, too, he sees, but rarely anything but the best. The theatre and the opera are as much his world as the woods, as his criticisms show. All this time he is writing frequently for *Forest and Stream*, the *Portland Transcript*, the *Nevada Territorial Enterprise*, and the *Newport News*. And yet he works always eleven hours a day in the store, and often fifteen or sixteen.

He writes exceedingly well. His letters to the *News* develop a true journalistic aptitude for picking out the salient and interesting features of the city. He writes of its

---

[82] Henry Denman Thompson (1833-1911) was a playwright and actor most famous for his 1875 sketch entitled, *Joshua Whitcomb*, a play about a New Hampshire country bumpkin who travels to the big city. He later rewrote the sketch into the four-act play, *The Old Homestead*.

amusements, its beggars, its Chinese, its bloody sand-lot riots, in one of which he became unwillingly involved and got out only by his presence of mind.

The man who said that he "wrote like Charles Dickens" did not come far from the mark; these letters called "*Going Towards Sunset*"[83] have the charm and insight of Boz's "American Notes." His humor is light and effective; his pathos is pathos; he never bungles over his transitions; he sees with clearness and unerringly selects what is interesting. One accepts it with difficulty as the uncorrected copy of a laboring man who had no regular schooling; for there is style without mannerism, elevation without affectation, adequacy of treatment, and the cadences are those of a student of Elizabethan English.

David Libbey wrote verse also, but only casually, and usually in his lighter moods. He had not his sister Lydia's gift for metre, yet quite in Francois Villon's own spirit he writes a ballade of dead beauties, in which he inquires for Dido and Sappho, for Lais and "Helen the fair," and for "Egypt's proud queen" as familiarly as if this were the pastime of a scholar and not the diversion of a Maine river-driver.

- - -

What a treasure these poems would have been to have located. In Libbey's letters home during his war year, he often mentioned sending home poems. It could be those were his days of contemplation in verse.

---

[83] The editor has been unsuccessful in locating copies of the letters under this title.

PENOBSCOT

IN California, David Libbey had time for leisure. He is no longer beholden to the cycles of the seasons. The spring ice melt does not require driving knees, the thaw of the earth does not call for planting, the buzz of the bee for gathering honey in the summer, the cool days of fall the haying and the harvest, nor the call of the hunt. His work is steady, during daylight hours, requiring him to neither rise before the sun or camp out under the stars. This must have been some difference for him, and to it he adjusted superbly.

Working in a stationery store, he handled paper not by the quire, but the ream; unlike during the war, he had no shortage to worry about. With his observational mind, his past experiences, and his new surroundings he put his time into writing, and it was during his years in California and Nevada when he was most productive as a writer.

In this newly added chapter, three selections from Libbey's writing are included. The first on games laws, the second on the lynx, and the third on the Maine moose.

Certainly, Libbey was writing before he traveled to California, but during those years out west he wrote consistently. In the following article he explained the need for game laws and wardens. The topic was spurred on by his time in the Adirondacks and what he witnessed the summer he dug ship timber with his nephews. In the article, he calls out the market fishermen in the north woods of New York for their blatant violations.

- - -

GAME PROTECTION[84]

FROM the editor, *Forest And Stream*: A valued correspondent writes from Indian Lake, Adirondacks, complaining of the law-breaking in that section.

BUSINESS having called me into the famous old 'North Woods' last summer, I packed my trunk on a lovely June day, with bright anticipation of glorious sport in the intervals of labor. How carefully I selected my flies; how critically I examined my leaders; how lovingly I looked over my rod, with which so many of the speckled beauties have been taken from their liquid home in the water of the Pine Tree State! Shortly after my arrival, passing one day up the side of a pond four or five miles in extent, I noticed that a boat was anchored at the mouth of each spring brook that debouched into the pond, and the single occupant thereof was either quietly bait fishing or industriously whipping the water with rod and reel. I was amazed. What! do trout bite here in the middle of a July day, with the sun pouring down a flood of fiery rays into the sparkling waters? However, I was too far

---

[84] Game Protection, *Forest And Stream*, October 5, 1876, Vol. 7 No. 9 - 1876-1877, pgs. 137-138.

away to inquire, so I repressed my curiosity until a person informed me that each of these worthies had a *gill net* set nearby, and the fishing was only a blind!

My residence of two months in these woods has amply confirmed what I was then told. How often have I seen a man — I suppose I must *call* him a man — with a string of trout, expatiating on the sport he had with such, and such big ones; how they run out his hundred-feet of line several times before he succeeded in landing them; and all the time with the accursed net, with which he obtained every fish, in his pocket. His listeners would gather round him and pretend to believe it all; but when his back was turned someone would quietly remark, 'He caught them with a Porter fly!' A shout of laughter from the rest would evince their appreciation of the joke, a 'Porter fly' being, in Adirondack vernacular, a gill net.[85]

It is not to be inferred that all the residents here are guilty of this infernal practice. There are guides and others who greatly deplore it, but if asked why they do not enforce the law invariably answer that they would be burnt out of house and home, or their lives endangered. But they all hold it as a point of honor to conceal the facts, as far as possible, from visiting sportsmen. The scarcity of trout is occasioned by the wet, or the drought, or the heat, or the cold; any cause rather than the true one, as the guides fear if known it would cause a diminution in the number who yearly resort here for the purpose of enjoying the delights of trout fishing. Last summer, camping in my own State, I caught something over three-hundred trout, very few of which weighed less than a

---

[85] A net in which fish get snagged by their gills.

quarter of a pound; and that without taking scarcely an hour from my business.[86]

Here, in the Adirondacks, the result of my fishing has been two trout, one of them four inches long and the other six, both of which I returned to grow until they were large enough to fill the meshes of the inevitable net. I read with interest Piseco's experiences here the present summer, well knowing the cause of the scarcity of trout of which he complains.[87]

Knowing the stand which your journal has always taken for the preservation of game and fish in this country, I venture to suggest a way in which the extermination of trout, surely foreshadowed in this wilderness, might be avoided, and that is, by the appointment of fish wardens at a stated salary, without any interest in the fines collected, the whole of which should go to the State. Plenty of young men can be found to do the work at a very moderate salary. Being, then, officers of the law, simply doing their duty, without any interest in the money received from fines, they would be secure from violence. To attack an officer, backed by the majesty of the State law, is quite a different thing from assaulting a neighbor for informing against you, and taking money extorted from you by a fine.

It is proper to state that this wholesale netting of trout is caused by the demand to supply the hotel tables in Saratoga, and accordingly, as one recedes from that great resort of

---

[86] An important note, as Libbey went to the Adirondacks for business, the hard work of digging knees, and still he made time to enjoy the woods and waters.

[87] Another contributor who wrote on the decimation of trout in the Adirondacks.

fashionable folly into the northern portion of the wilderness, the practice nearly ceases, and fishing is consequently much better. Still, the headwaters and tributaries of Moose River, in the wildest and least frequented part of the Adirondacks, have been persistently raked through this whole season by parties who remained on the ground, an agent going in each week to carry in provisions and bring out the fish.

This article is already much too long, but I cannot close without referring to the absurd law which opens the season for grouse shooting on August 1st. It causes almost a feeling of horror in the breast of any true sportsman to see the slaughter of the tiny, half-fledged birds, many of them scarcely able to fly high enough to alight beyond the reach of the dog. When the mother of the brood is sacrificed, they convert her into a 'chicken partridge' by simply pulling out her tail feathers. This practice also is carried on to furnish 'game suppers' to the pleasure seekers of Saratoga, 'chicken partridges' being their greatest delicacy.[88]

Penobscot.
Indian Lake, N. Y., Sept. 6th.

---

[88] The open season on grouse in New York (and Maine) is now later in the year. Check local Game Laws and dates.

THE LOUP CERVIER

LIBBEY wrote this next article for *Forest and Stream*, while living out West. The essay shows his passion for educating the hunter and the general reader on wildlife.[89]

In the story, Libbey describes an exhibit he viewed at the Centennial Exposition. Based on an animal display there, he was able to identify cats once trapped in Maine that were unknown to even an experienced woodsman and trader.

- - -

A GREAT deal of confusion has arisen in regard to the characteristics of this animal, or shall we say animals, owing to the fact that the earlier writers confounded the Canada Lynx with the wolverene. Thirty years ago, when the wolverene was plentiful in almost every part of Maine, and was quite destructive to young lambs, it was scarcely ever called anything else than "wolverine;" in fact, the trapper's name for the animal today is "wolvin," which anyone can see is only an abbreviation of the former name. It was only a short time since that the writer read an account in a Maine local paper of a stage team being badly frightened by a wild "animal," which was claimed to be a "wolverene," meaning of course a lynx as the wolverene is not found in any part of the State.

It is the writer's opinion that the name "Loup cervier" was not given by the early French voyagers to the lynx, but to the

---

[89] *Lynxes. The Loup Cervier, Or Canada Lynx. Forest and Stream.* V13, 1879-1880.

wolverene, as the name loses all significance when applied to the lynx, and genuine hunters would never be guilty of the absurdity of calling an animal a "deer-wolf," which has all the characteristics of a cat, and preys on nothing larger than a rabbit.

It is true that Hearne, or Richardson — I forget which — speaks of the animal gathering a kind of moss which deer are very fond of, piling it up at the foot of a tree, provided with a convenient limb overhead for the animal to crouch on, and when the unsuspecting victim approaches to feast on the dainty repast so generously provided, dropping down on to its back, and cutting its throat with its sharp fangs. But this is precisely what is said of the wolverene and of no other animal, and the writer alluded to seems to have been misled by a confusion of names.

The lynx has nearly disappeared from the lower and central portion of Maine, but abounds in the vast forests of the northern border. It cares but little for the presence of man, and the writer once saw a very large one shot in broad daylight within four rods of a camp door, where it was unconcernedly feasting on the offal of an ox, slaughtered there the day before. It must, however, have been greatly pressed by hunger, as it is essentially a nocturnal animal. Its huge cushioned feet surrounded by a thick fringe of hair enable it to walk on the surface of any but the lightest kind of snow, and it is an expert in the capture of the hare. Where these abound, it has a curious habit of catching them, apparently for sport, sometimes leaving them where killed, and again hiding them, as if for future consumption. It is silent, except during the pairing season, which occurs in March. Then during the night, and sometimes in thick, stormy days, it gives utterance to a variety of cries and calls, all more or less feline, and one almost exactly resembling the "Miau" of a huge tom cat. They are exceedingly active, and are capable of making tremendous bounds, but cannot keep up an extended fight, and are easily treed by a dog, when one can be found to run the trail, which is not often. They leave scarcely a vestige of any trail, but are so very cat-like in all their movements that their earlier designation of *Felis canadensis* seems more appropriate, though perhaps less scientific than their later one of *Lynx borealis*.[90]

The animal is almost as easily trapped as a dog, and the best skins command about $2.50. But a few years ago they were made the subject of a curious speculation. The skins were artificially colored by furriers, made into sets, and sold as "Black Lynx." They took amazingly, and became at once the fashion; the raw skins trebled in price, while mink, which they superseded, suffered a corresponding depression. This lasted for two seasons, and then there was a sudden collapse. Even the votaries of fashion refused any longer to purchase an article of which the color, fur, and skin were equally worthless. As the first faded, the second was coarse and came out easily, and the last was almost as tender as a rabbit's.

The other representative of the family, the bay lynx, is somewhat rare in Maine, and is called by hunters "wild cat" and "bob cat." I believe this to be the animal so frequently spoken of as being killed in different sections of the New England States while engaged in robbing hen roosts, etc.,

---

[90] Taxonomy has changed over time. *Felis canadensis* was a 1792 proposal. Even as recent as the early 2000s, scientists were divided over whether Lynx should be considered a subgenus of Felis, or a subfamily itself.

though it is often called (*mistakenly*) a Canada lynx. The latter animal, in my opinion, is never found at any great distance from caves, and is best at home where the wilderness is vastest; but the bay lynx is found in the lower portion of the State, in small forests surrounded by fields. What strengthens my belief that it is often called the Canada lynx is the fact that this animal is shown in the pictorial illustrations in *Webster's Unabridged*[91] as a veritable wild cat, with a ringed tail six inches in length at least, and the only difference one can detect between that and the bay lynx, as depicted in Webster's, is simply a change in position! This mistake in the illustration would readily be seen by anyone familiar with the western bay lynx, for this animal is so totally different in color and markings, and so insignificant in size, as compared with its Maine namesake, that no person of common sense would ever dream of calling the two animals the same.

Let me illustrate by a single anecdote in point. In 1875, an old trapper caught two of the western variety in the northern part of Maine, and never having seen anything like them, he brought them out just as they were caught – that is unskinned. None of his friends would name them, and he took them to a well-known fur dealer and sportsman. After a long examination the dealer pronounced them a pair of half-grown kittens, a cross between the bay and Canada lynx, and had them carefully skinned and mounted as curiosities.[92] And such they certainly were, being the first and last of their kind that were ever seen in the State.

---

[91] An old edition from the 1800s.

[92] See note in the inset at the end of this chapter.

The writer saw them after being mounted, but never having seen the western lynx at that time, was as much in the dark in regard to their true character as all the rest. But the following season, on going into the Kansas and Nebraska State Building, in the Centennial grounds, he was confounded on seeing their exact counterpart, labeled *the bay lynx*. Since then he has seen scores, all alike as two peas — light gray, with brown spots. There is not a gray hair in the Maine variety, except a narrow strip underneath. It is a very dark reddish brown, with black spots; and it is no exaggeration to say that the Maine species could pick up and carry off the western lynx as easily as a cat could carry a kitten.

- Penobscot.

- - -

If the meaning of "Loup cervier" was corrupted, that occurred as far back as 1879, and as of the year 2022, most online dictionaries equate *Loup cervier* with the Canada lynx. From Latin, *Lupus cervārius* might translate to 'wolf that hunts deer'; and cerva translates to doe. The word *cervine*, means to resemble or have the characteristic of deer; or to be deerlike. The word derivations indicate that *Loup cervier* may have originally applied an animal that was wolf-like and preyed on deer. The Canada lynx has not shown the capability of preying on full-sized, healthy deer, unless in times of extreme hunger, and it certainly is not a wolf-like animal. While an adult Canada Lynx may prey on small fawns, or injured mature deer, the main diet of this cat is much smaller animals, and typically rabbits.

The following table has been compiled from articles of the 1800s and papers of Manly Hardy and David Libbey, who were two of the foremost authorities on Maine animals of their day. It seems the common naming of a few of these animals has been causing confusion for two-hundred years.[93]

---

[93] For a paper by Manly Hardy on this topic, see, *Katahdin, Pamola, & Whiskey Jack – Stories and Legends from The Maine Woods*, Burnt Jacket Publishing, (2021).

Species	Main diet
Panther *Felis concolor* *Catamount, Cougar, Puma,* *Mountain Lion*	When they existed in Maine they preyed on deer, caribou, and moose; smaller animals when necessary.
Wolverine *Gulo luscus* *Carcarjou; wolvin; Indian* *devil; lunksoos; lucivee;* *glutton; skunk bear;* *quickhatch; (Possibly the* *original animal to which* *'Loup cervier' was applied* *according to Libbey).*	Deer, rabbits, rodents, and even scavengers, eating the carrion (carcasses) left by wolves.
Canada Lynx *Felis canadensis (1972)* *Lynx borealis* (Canada) *Lynx canadensis* *Loup cervier*	Snowshoe hares, hares, squirrels, small rodents, grouse. A trapper saying goes, *"A good rabbit year, is sure to bring a good lynx year."*
Bobcat *Lynx Roux* *Lynx rufus (ruffus)* *Red lynx* Bay Lynx, or lynx cat, is a hybrid species that is a cross between Lynx Roux and the Lynx of Canada.	Hares, squirrels, small rodents, grouse. Domestic chickens. *(The cat furs Libbey observed both in Maine and at the Centennial Exposition. There may have been a distinguishing factor Libbey observed between the eastern and mid-western variety of the time.)*

This table is not the definitive summary as regional names applied to species, and habitat conditions will dictate prey selection over time. The three larger cats noted will all prey on deer when the snow is deep giving them the advantage.

THE MAINE MOOSE

IN the most unlikely of places, a second-floor window in San Francisco reminds David Libbey of the majestic moose. The display he sees prompts him to write the following article to lend what he knows about the moose and the deer.

- - -

THE MOOSE
(*Alces alces americanus* – or *americana*)
(From, *Woods and Lakes of Maine – Annotated Edition.*
Burnt Jacket Publishing, 2020.)

HABITS AND PECULIARITIES OF THE MOOSE[94]

THERE is probably no animal on this continent about which so little that is strictly true is publicly known, and so much that is false or absurd has been written, as the one whose name stands at the head of this article.

No stronger proof of the first assertion is needed than a glance at the two great lexicons to which Americans are accustomed to flee for information. Webster gives a cut of the European and American elk, with a description which leaves the reader to infer that the latter animal and the moose are identical; while Worcester has a representation of a nondescript animal, which is neither the one nor the other, with a description of the "elk" or "moose" extracted from the *British Cyclopedia.* The *New American Cyclopedia* has a very full and correct description of the forms and appearance of the moose, but says: "a male, female and fawn usually yard together," and speaks of the animal as "tramping down the snow in its yard," both of which assertions are utterly at variance with the facts. Now as the utter extermination of the moose in this country is only a question of time, it is important that its habits should be thoroughly understood during its existence.[95]

---

[94] Habits and Peculiarities of the Moose, Forest and Stream, Vol. 8, No. 3, Feb 22, 1877.

[95] While the caribou, wolf, wolverine, and catamount were expatriated from Maine, the moose, thankfully due to Game Laws and a properly defined hunting season, survived the prediction he made.

It is an extremely shy and solitary animal, making its haunt in the deepest recesses of the forest. The early writers evidently obtained their knowledge of it at second hand. One of them speaks of it as "invariably browsing backwards," and that it is hunted in the following manner:

"The hunter creeps on the track with the greatest caution till he discovers by the marks on the snow that he is very near it. He then "breaks a twig, at which sound the moose starts up and prepares to flee, when the hunter fires and seldom fails to bring down his game."

Nothing more absurd could well be written. Fancy a moose browsing backwards in three feet of snow, with a stiff crust on the top! How can the hunter tell by the "marks on the snow" that he is very near it? and why is the animal invariably lying down at that particular moment? It is true that the experienced still hunter can tell about how long a time has elapsed since the passage of the animal by drawing his finger across the "drag" made in the snow when withdrawing its feet, except when the snow and air are at the same temperature, when this sign fails. But even when in force it cannot be depended on as indicating the proximity of the animal, as it may have been lying down for hours, or, on the contrary, it may have been startled by some unusual sound in the forest, at a point just beyond that to which the hunter has arrived, and be already miles away, when the hunter supposes it to be within gunshot.

Strolling up California Street the other evening, I caught sight through an opposite window in the second story of a building, just occupied by a traveling museum, of the antlers of the noble game under consideration. I paid my "two bits" and passed up the stairs, where I found myself in the presence of a stuffed specimen of a "bull moose" about four years old, suspended from whose neck was a placard bearing the following remarkable legend! *"Swiftest animal on earth; has been known to trot 17 miles an hour for 24 hours; never known to gallop."*

To give color to this extraordinary assertion the taxidermist, in mounting the skin, had stretched it to nearly twice its normal length, with a corresponding diminution in size, and had drawn its hind legs backward till it bore about the same relation to the living animal that a thoroughbred greyhound does to an English bull dog. By dint of questioning, the fact was elicited that the animal was shot somewhere on the Columbia River a little more than a year ago. There was no appearance of any "bell" hanging from the throat, and a close inspection failed to discover any signs of its having been cut off; but it is hardly probable that the animal differs so essentially from its congener of the Atlantic slope.[96] But the false ideas conveyed by that ridiculous placard will be carried away, and be rehearsed by the readers to children and "children's children."

The moose is not a remarkably swift animal. The writer once saw a freshly started one strike out on to an open bay over a mile in extent, where the footing was perfect, he just sinking enough to steady his feet. He was pursued by two dogs of ordinary speed, who not only found no difficulty in keeping up with him, but would repeatedly dart across in the

---

[96] The 'bell' or dewlap is present on both male and female moose. The point Libbey was making here was that the specimen was billed as a bull moose, and he saw no evidence of the bell. Surely an oddity to mention.

vain endeavor to seize upon his heels, losing thereby several rods of ground, which they easily regained.

That for which the animal is remarkable is his long continued powers of endurance, and his apparent indifference to, and ability to overcome, any natural obstruction in his native wilds. He not only surmounts with ease, and without breaking his trot, windfalls over six feet in height, but he also passes over with impunity the most treacherous and bottomless morasses.[97] Indeed, half his existence in the summer season, when undisturbed, is passed in the latter, feeding on the stalks and roots of the yellow water lily, which is above all his favorite food.

Almost all writers speak of his tramping down the snow in his yard, and many write of the hard-beaten paths made by the animals in going and returning to their yards, as if they left them in the morning and returned at night like cattle to a corral. The size of the yarding ground is regulated wholly and solely by two considerations— the depth and hardness of the snow, and the facilities for browsing. When the snow is shallow and soft they will wander forward for miles, hardly ever straight forward, but beating back and forth over more or less width of ground, usually on each side of a brook of open mountain water. When the snow becomes very deep, or a sharp crust is formed on the top of it, their field of operation is correspondingly restricted. They will then retrace their steps carefully, walking in the paths already made, and eating the coarsest food they daintily rejected when travel was unimpeded. Sometimes, when the fearful

---

[97] A morass is a tract of wet ground such as, a marsh, a swamp, or a bog.

northern snows come down in depths of six feet, and the sun of March forms a crust on which a man can travel without often breaking through, it is almost impossible for them to move sufficiently to avoid starvation. They will then eat every green thing as high as they can reach, and which is not more than an inch in diameter, and such places where they are thus "snowed up" can be told at a glance by the experienced hunter for years afterward.

The two sexes never yard together of their own volition. Sometimes a male will be chased into a yard of females or *vice versa*, and its track be lost by mingling with those that cross and recross it in every direction. Then, if the snow is deep or the crust sharp, it will remain there, always, however, choosing a part abandoned by its former occupants, and which they thereafter always carefully avoid. To such an extent is the avoidance of the sexes carried during the winter season that the young male invariably separates from his mother the second fall (when 18 months old), and sometimes even the first, as the writer has found them in yards with older males when less than a year old. The females, on the contrary, remain with their dams[98] two and three years. So that it is not unusual to find the mother, her first, second and third offspring, and one of her eldest in the same yard. This is the extent of their breeding together. My observations teach me that they are less gregarious than any other variety of the Cervidae.[99]

---

[98] *Dam* was a term used for the female parent of an animal; variant of dame.

[99] The family of animals that include the deer, elk, moose, and related forms. Note: the scientific name for the moose is *Alces*

The first young is dropped at two years of age, only one the first birth and often the second; after that two, and I believe always of opposite sexes— at least I have never seen an exception, and the same is true of the common deer. When three are dropped at a birth they are usually, if not always, two females and a male; one of the females is undoubtedly incapable of reproduction, as in no other way can the presence of "barren does" be reasonably accounted for. They bear about the same proportion to the whole numbers as do the number of triple births. They appear to be perfect animals in all their parts, are somewhat stouter and more compactly built than their fruitful companions, and all invariably loaded down with fat in August, when those having fawns are quite lean. I am speaking now of deer, as my opportunities for observing them have been so much greater, but it applies equally to moose, so far as I have been able to judge.[100]

But to return to our mutton (or venison).

---

alces americana. It is said the word *moose* comes from the Algonquin word 'moosu' meaning 'bark stripper.'

[100] Since David Libbey's well-thought out observations, there have been many studies by biologists on deer and moose populations. As a point of illustration, a 2017 paper, *Reproductive characteristics of female white-tailed deer (Odocoileus virginianus) in the Midwestern USA*, Green, et. al., in Theriogenology Vol. 94, May 2017, Pg. 71-78, found: 1) a mean litter size among all pregnant females was 1.9 fetuses, 2) Longitudinally, over the years studied they found a 1:1 male to female birth rate. This last fact is quite remarkable, for year to year the researchers found differences in the ratio, but 1:1 on average, and so Libbey must have naturally averaged his observations over time for his accurate conclusions.

The food of the moose in summer consists of the various tender grasses and plants springing up on the low bottoms and banks of streams, and the lily mentioned above. In winter it is governed wholly by the temperature. In the coldest weather they retire to the almost impenetrable thickets, and subsist solely on the fine boughs of the evergreens — fir, cedar and hemlock — the first being decidedly their favorite, while the cedar is greatly preferred by deer. This taste for the evergreens is a wise provision designed by Providence for their preservation, as the heat generated by fermentation in their stomachs is undoubtedly what enables them to withstand the effects of the intense cold. When the weather softens they immediately leave their coverts and repair to the sides of the ridges and upland water courses, where they subsist exclusively on hardwood browse — that is, the twigs of deciduous trees, the "moosewood" and "whitewood" (two varieties of the maple) being their favorites. The mode of browsing by is so radically different from that of the females that an old hunter can tell at once, on finding a yard, which sex inhabits it, even if the tracks are obliterated.

The bulls will approach a tree three inches in circumference, and seizing it as high up as they can reach with their prehensile upper lip and sharp under teeth, will force it downwards until they can get their fore leg over it, when they will commence browsing off it, standing astride it, and gradually working their way to the top, which having devoured at their leisure they will leave it to spring back, looking as though a hurricane had passed over it. It is held by the majority of intelligent hunters that a bull moose never gnaws the bark of a tree, in which belief I fully concur. In all cases coming under my observation, where it was claimed they had done so, it was evidently done by cows before the yarding season. They are much more delicate feeders than the males, never pulling down the trees, and contenting themselves with the finest of the browse, and gnawing the bark off the standing poplars and maples on one side, but rarely or never going round it, so that it is seldom killed, but slowly grows over, showing the marks for years; and there are townships in my native State where one can travel the day through and scarcely be out of sight of trees thus mutilated twenty years ago. These noble animals fairly swarmed in all upper portions of the State. Their destruction is a matter of history.[101]

Space and time are both too valuable for the discussion of such an unprofitable subject.

The being with the skin and clothes of a white man, who in one winter butchered seventy-five of them for their hides alone, leaving their meat to pollute the air, still flourishes on the upper waters of the Passadumkeag, and a few months ago, after bringing a party of nine sportsmen with twelve or fifteen dogs from Rhode Island, who were obliged to go back in a hurry to avoid prosecution, he came out with a communication in a leading State paper deprecating the law which forbids deer hunting with dogs, on the ground that sportsmen left twenty dollars in the State for every deer they took out! His memory deserves to be execrated more than him who burned the celebrated temple of antiquity, for

---

[101] See earlier note. The largest threat to moose in Maine at this time is not over-hunting, but the winter tick.

destroyed temples can be rebuilt, but exterminated species cannot be recreated.[102]

> \- Penobscot.
> San Francisco, Jan. 22d, 1877.

---

[102] See, *Exploring the Maine Woods – The Hardy Family Expedition to the Machias Lakes*, and the reference to Jock Darling that Libbey is making in these statements. It is interesting to note that upon the death of Jock Darling, who was labeled as an *Outlaw of the Maine Woods*, David Libbey reportedly came to his defense, at least according to one author. In the essay, "Jock Darling: The Notorious "Outlaw" of the Maine Woods," James Vickery (2002) called Libbey *a friend* of Darling's, and referenced an article in the Bangor Daily Commercial where Libbey supposedly wrote, *"to call Jock Darling an outlaw would be an insult to his memory."* The implication Vickery alludes to from this statement, supposedly from Libbey, is that Darling market hunted like many of the mid-1800s before the newer game laws. If Darling had revised his ways, and was following the game laws, then this would have been true. However, the evidence points to Darling's continued breaking of the laws, even if he was framed in the end. The editor continues to search for the original article in the *Bangor Daily Commercial* referenced by Vickery to review the specific letter from Libbey. As of publication, no library search has been able to find an issue with such a letter from Libbey, and neither is it included with the James Vickery Papers housed at the University of Maine Fogler Library.

ON TO NEVADA

IN the spring of 1878, Hodge & Co., the San Francisco stationery store, became insolvent, and in April, Libbey looked up another job. It was an entirely new departure for him when he engaged to go into the deserts of Nevada to make boracic acid from the borax beds there. The location was less than a hundred miles north of the now famous Death Valley.[103]

His employer was an aged, eccentric, and irritable character, and worse, for he was an amateur at his business. His associate a Chinaman with whom he had little in common. His home much of the time was a dug-out in the side of a natural mound. There was no drinking-water within four and a half miles, no ranch within eight, no woman within thirteen, nothing but coyotes and the desert, "truly a God-forsaken hole," he writes.

---

[103] The borax beds of Nevada drove many to the region for work and the abundant supply of borax. In the late 1800s and into the early 20th century, boron compounds from these borax beds, were a household staple. The products were used in medicines, food additives, household cleaners, detergents, cosmetics and many other products. Mule teams were used to transport the boric acid from the deserts to the train and onward to the factories. Between 1964–65, before turning politician, one of President Ronald Reagan's television roles was as the host of *Death Valley Days,* a show sponsored by Pacific Coast Borax Company depicting the American West.

The work was a failure from the start. The whole episode falls just enough short of being tragedy to read like farce.

- May 25. Griffing began cooking, crystallizing borate of lime and soda between meals! He can make it by the ounce well enough, but can't make it by the ton. However, he believes his failure wholly due to the character of the stuff dug here, notwithstanding the fact that he had nearly eight tons from Fish Lake which he used with the rest, getting in all less than 600 pounds of boracic acid, I should judge, and using 1800 pounds of sulfuric acid! In my opinion he is in his dotage and ought to have a guardian.

- - -

- June 4. Having lived for nearly a week without bread, Griffing being unequal to the task of making it, I made a batch tonight, having all along played ignorance of cooking to avoid the responsibility. But he starved me out!

- June 24. Griffing discharged me this morning, very coolly saying that he would send me the money when he got it. Naturally I refused to be discharged in *that* fashion and finally we came to an amicable understanding.

- July 9. Griffing concluded that the operation was a failure and made up his mind to quit and sell off his stuff, but he said he was going to use up the other tank of sulfuric acid first, as he could not sell it. As he cannot make boracic acid enough to pay Sam's and my wages, not counting the sulfuric acid, it shows how much sense he has or how little!

- July 17. Griffing has a spasm of common-sense; drew off water, shoveled out acid and threw it away!

After this he sold out and does not appear again in the story except when he "balanced account by charging the same order twice."

Immediately after, Libbey gets work in a foundry, in place of an ill-conditioned and intemperate carpenter. He has a roving commission, — making flasks, pounding iron, mending wagons; he upholsters a sofa, papers rooms, makes a pig-pen, the circle for a buggy, the pattern for a cooking-range, window sashes, a stump-machine toggle, and so on. He now lives sumptuously in an adobe hut lined with drilling to keep the dirt from sifting down.

Still, in spite of having cast off his Old Man of the Sea, his days are not altogether free from anxieties. There is Hull, the carpenter, whom he had displaced.

- July 29. Hull, alias Chips, the man I superseded at the foundry, invited me to his cabin, lent me five hollow and round planes, and then showed me a four-barrel pepper-box revolver, saying, 'There are one or two fellows I am going to shoot if they do not leave me alone.'

The journal implies a childish confidence in Hull's good intentions. David Libbey's son says, on the contrary, that his father perfectly well understood that Hull intended to kill him. Wholly unarmed, he tamed the man as he would have tamed a wild animal. He never took his eye off Hull, yet he showed no suspicion; and the charm of his conversation, coupled with his fearlessness, finally won him the good-will of his would-be slayer, so that they "parted with a hearty hand-clasp."

- July 30. Hull fulfilled his word by shooting D. Holland.
- July 31. 90 degrees. Holland died about 3 p.m. Began to make him a coffin.
- Aug. 24. The sheriff arrived this eve with Chips, catching him at Wadsworth.

It is interesting to meet Chips once more; for, from reasons not recorded, that appearance with the sheriff was not final. Evidently, he remained the friend of David Libbey.

- - -

The next journal note Eckstorm included is from five months later. Also of interest is how Chips is *not* incarcerated for his crime.

- - -

- Jan 27. Chips gave me a letter from a French lady named Flaherty, who wants a job done on her house at Pick-handle Gulch, Candelaria.[104] As Chips dares not go there for fear of the vengeance of the Northern Belle miners for the slaying of Holland, he turns the job over to me.

Investigation did not enamor Libbey of either Pick-handle Gulch or "the French lady named Flaherty," though he went and saw both; but the little record is like a lost story by Bret Harte.[105] What a rich humor of grotesqueness envelops the

---

[104] Near Candelaria Mountain, Nevada.

[105] The short story writer mentioned in an earlier footnote.

whole situation — the names, the grouping, the field of action, the atmosphere, the romantic French lady, the affable murderer, the miners thirsting for their revenge.

Nevada was not effetely quiescent in those days; the bullets flew occasionally.

- Dec. 27. Had a shooting scrape in the boarding-house at supper, McFarland and his China cook taking a shot apiece at each other, unhappily without effect.

This he writes nonchalantly. Libbey never went armed himself, saying that he distrusted the quickness of his own temper. Nevertheless, a man brought up in the Maine woods, as he had been, was not to be despised as a "tenderfoot," and at times he proved a trifle disconcerting even to the typical Western "bad man." As, for example, when an armed and drunken desperado insulted him in a saloon and, without hesitation, Libbey sprang upon the man.

Libbey's son told Eckstorm the story:

"Father put one fist under the fellow's chin, drew back the other and threatened to drive him through the wall if he opened his mouth. After recovering from his surprise, the fellow meekly asked for permission to speak."

The journal characteristically forgets to mention the incident.

So far David Libbey's Western experience had been a hard one; but better luck was before him. At length he got into the business of setting up mining machinery, which was both satisfactory and profitable. Incidentally he learned much about extracting silver and something of gold-mining. If it were not a palpable fallacy that the man who can do every part of the work can also do the whole work, we might assert that David Libbey could make the patterns and castings for his own machinery, assemble them and set up his machines, build the mill that covered them, the railroad track which brought the ore, the crusher which crushed it; could manage and repair his own steam-engines; manage, clean and keep in repair his silver batteries and extract the silver himself. Thus, not only doing every part of the work connected with the extraction of ore, but also making his mills and all his machinery. His journals show that he had done all this in detail at different times. Not until we consider his proficiency in many other trades and their great diversity, do we appreciate the capabilities of such a man.

It is in this last portion of his Western experience that fortune really smiles upon him. He is able to command high wages for his work and to get more than he can do. There are no more Griffings, with their tempers, their inefficiency, their obstinacy — and their book-keeping! He is kept busy enlarging mills, setting up new machinery, changing from one style of crusher to another, doing work which one wonders at, knowing that he never learned the trade of machinist.

His sufficient success enables him to make a handsome retreat and to go back to his own home in Maine, where he arrived March 20, 1880, three years and six months after leaving.

- - -

Why after leaving San Francisco, Libbey did not immediately return home to Maine is an unanswered question.

ONCE AGAIN AT HOME

AFTER his return to Maine, David Libbey took up again his old pursuits among his old friends. Too old to follow the river as a driver any longer, he turned again to getting out ship timber and knees. He hunted every year as before, but now he hunted for home use only. The old love of the chase was as strong as ever in him. The woods were his pleasure-ground; he never tired of them. His journals, fuller than ever before, were rich in materials; his observation, better trained, was keener; his memory did not fail him; he was accumulating treasures of wood-lore. But space forbids trenching ever so little upon the events of the last twenty-five years of his life. It is enough that they were peaceful, happy years, without great incidents or upheavals, along the lines of the years already delineated.

Space also forbidding any mention of his published writings, it is impossible to show one side of his life which has not been touched on, that of the naturalist, the man who studied the creatures he lived among.[106]

"He used to talk to the animals in the woods and to the bees in a way peculiar to him," writes his daughter, "because I have seen the effect upon animals, and he would pick up a little fawn and carry it under his arm."

---

[106] In this edition, several essays follow from David Libbey that provide his knowledge of nature and wildlife.

Every detail of anything he had once seen was photographed upon his memory with a vividness which suffered no loss by time. To recall an incident was like taking out the photographic negatives of every successive stage of it, I have met but two other men who had the power in at all the same degree, and both were woodsmen.[107]

As his son once said to me:

"I went to Father's memory as to a book for anything I wanted; he opened to the page and read it off; and I never thought of the book being all his own, to be lost with him."

And again:

"Father had a marvelous eye for topography. When he went through thick woods, it was as if he had a bird's-eye view of the whole region; he knew how the woods lay and the waters ran, and he never forgot it." Now, this is not memory in the accepted sense; it is an unconscious registering of facts which are held without effort and indefinitely, — a peculiar relation to the subliminal self.

THERE are several of Libbey's articles that detail his observations of wildlife. In his younger years, the skill Libbey had as a hunter was necessary to provide for his family. As he aged, his writing shows he aimed to explain the habits of animals, his appreciation for them, and the

---

[107] One of these men was surely her own father, Manly Hardy.

necessary conservation to ensure future generations would also get to experience the wonder of the woods.

A common theme of Libby's articles are responses to inaccuracies in other's contributions. In fact, many letters to publications at the time were often one outdoorsman correcting another's observations or conclusions. This isn't that much different than today's sportsmen. One thing we can be sure of, the animal world is full of different, peculiar, and wonderful behaviour; just when you think you know what a species will do, they go and prove you wrong.

For his part, David Libbey was a woodsman-writer to be trusted for his contributions. When he wrote that he observed a certain behaviour or condition in the woods, the readers could be sure he was retelling it accurately. His next essay is on the drumming of the ruffed grouse, a sound quiet stalkers of the woods may have heard, but very few are able to get close enough to see the bird in action.

HABITS OF THE RUFFED GROUSE[108]

I READ, doubtless in common with thousands of your readers, Mr. Whitehead's article on Grouse, in *Scribner's*, and noticed the inaccuracy of his statement that they strut up and down a log and beat it with their wings. But it strikes me that Mr. Murdock, in his strictures on the article, commits far greater errors than those he seeks to correct. It is true that the bird does not always select a hollow log, but that he frequently does so I can testify. I have found them on pines four feet in diameter, and as hollow as a barrel. I have also

---

[108] Forest and Stream, Vol. 9, No. 8. (1877-1878).

seen them drum on the root of a standing tree, and once shot one off a huge granite boulder. But these are exceptions. Ninety-nine out of every hundred select a fallen tree, and almost always a pine, even where hemlock and other down trees are more numerous. As for the statement that the grouse will drum "wherever he happens to be," nothing could well be more at variance with the facts.

When wholly undisturbed in his native woods, the grouse returns to the same log year after year; and in the wilds of Maine, where brood after brood is reared without ever seeing the face of man, I have seen drumming logs which bore the appearance of having been used for that purpose for a quarter of a century. But the bird has a wonderful faculty of adapting itself to the changes which are necessary for self-preservation in the vicinity of civilization; and near villages, where scarcely a day passed without their being hunted by troops of boys.

I have known one of these birds to have half a dozen drumming logs, running or flying from one to the other, and never drumming twice successively on the same log. This very precaution might prove its destruction, as it would only be necessary to wait at one of the logs till he visited it in turn; but, fortunately for the bird's preservation, the average American boy is not a very close observer of nature, and does not discover the trick. In regard to its drumming not being a love call, I have only to say that in more than a score of instances I have seen the female fly directly to the log to join the male; as well as witnessing two desperate fights between the drummer and an intruder; the female, meanwhile, sitting placidly by within twenty feet of the combatants.

I also know of two females shot while drumming, in a case of mistaken identity. From one log I had shot at what I thought was a male, and two mornings subsequent the same thing had been done by a companion, as I afterward learned to another female. Although I have repeatedly known the females to do the same thing since, I never repeated the blunder, as I speedily learned to distinguish the female drumming from that of the male, it being performed with much less precision; rather a sort of fluttering several times repeated.

As for autumn drumming, I have shot scores— I might almost say hundreds — of them while thus engaged, and have always found the birds shot to be young males. The explanation has always seemed to me very simple: The bird has reached maturity, its sexual instincts are awakened, and it drums, before learning the proper season, which goes to prove it a "love note" instead of operating against it, else they would drum at all seasons. In regard to their night drumming, I have observed that it takes place either in very dark, foggy or drizzly nights, or in the brightest moonlight, as when the glorious harvest moon of October floods the forest glades with a radiance almost equal to the light of day. In the former instance I have always supposed that the bird was belated, and unable to reach its roosting ground, owing to the sudden approach of darkness, and in the latter was deceived by the brightness of the moon.

I now wish to notice a remarkable habit indulged in by certain males of this species at rare intervals, and which has never to my knowledge been noticed by any naturalist. Once, while partridge hunting when a mere boy, I descried at some distance ahead of me, in an old "logging road," a strange looking bird, apparently without head or tail, and almost perfectly round in appearance. To shoot it was the work of an instant, and running to get it I was almost petrified with astonishment to pick up an ordinary cock partridge.

I was acquainted with an old hunter, a close observer of the habits of all kinds of game, and to him I went with my story. He informed me that what I had seen and shot was a "King Partridge;" that in forty years of hunting he had only seen three or four, and that years would probably elapse before I would see another. It was quite true; it was at least ten years; and in the meantime, I had grown to man's estate and had discarded my shotgun for a rifle and was deer hunting "on the leaves" one October when I next saw the "King Partridge." This time, you may be sure, I did not fire at it, but crept cautiously as near as I thought prudent without alarming the bird. The more I looked at it, the greater became my curiosity, and I determined to see what effect my appearance would have on it. I therefore stepped out in plain sight. As it paid not the slightest attention to me, I walked within twenty feet of it and examined it at my leisure. Every feather was perfectly erect, pointing if anything, forward of a perpendicular. The tail was spread out to its utmost extent, and laid forward almost flat on its back. Its neck was drawn in, so that when the bird was viewed, en profile, its head was entirely invisible, its ruff extending far beyond it. Its wings were slightly extended and drooping, so that the points just touched the leaves, and about every half minute it made a little dart forward about two feet, exactly like an old gobbler except that it hopped with both feet like a robin, and during the two hours in which I chased it round I could not get it to move in any other manner. There were half a dozen more ordinary grouse, male and female, in the flock, all of which had retired to a safe distance on my approach, leaving their "king" alone. He was very loth to take wing, but by running up and actually kicking so near as to nearly touch him, I forced him to take flight several times. He would fly about ten rods, and on alighting immediately assume the same position. After, I submitted him to a careful examination. His plumage was remarkably profuse and perfect, the ruff very large and glossy, showing beautifully green in the sunlight; the tail one-fourth longer than in ordinary birds, and showing reddish bars across it instead of the lighter colors usually seen; but I have frequently shot them, having the same peculiarity.

I have seen two more since then; one only two years ago, which, after following it around for nearly three hours, with exactly the same results as I have already described, I left in peace, not having the heart to kill it. I have only to add that I have given a perfectly faithful description without the slight exaggeration, having in fact an utter contempt for any person who willfully attempts to mislead in matters pertaining to natural history.

- Penobscot.
San. Francisco, Sept. 7, 1877.

POLING UP THE RAPIDS

(From, *Woods and Lakes of Maine – Annotated Edition*. Burnt Jacket Publishing, 2020.)

PICKEREL PROBLEMS

WHEN writing about Libbey's childhood, Eckstorm mentioned two articles David wrote later in his life. The first was a mention of his trout trophy. His second was on his bear encounter and the full essay was included earlier. In this article we have the full fish story, and in addition he provides a clear argument to the true enemy of the trout.

This essay is one of Libbey's longest to be added to this edition. In this piece we find an outdoorsman-writer who is an expert on the fisheries of Maine, and other locations as well. The casual reader, who may not be interested in the battle between pickerel and trout may be tempted to skip this chapter. However, the writing includes interesting historical notations on places in Maine along the Penobscot River and up to the Moosehead Lake region. In addition, Libbey provides an itinerary describing a trip up the East Branch of the Penobscot, providing a perspective on the woods, lakes and rivers that should not be missed.

DO PICKEREL DESTROY TROUT[109]

IN fancy I can see the derisive smile which will overspread the countenance of every angler who reads the above caption. Do pickerel destroy trout, forsooth! Are they not the scourge

---

[109] *Forest And Stream*, May 22, 1879.

of our inland ponds? The sharks of our streams and rivers? And forty years ago did not trout abound in thousands of brooks and ponds where they are now wholly exterminated by these voracious monsters?

Softly, my friends! It has been a little more than forty years since the writer, then a "barefoot boy," drew his first trout (a three-pounder) from the sparkling waters of the Sebois, just where it joins the Piscataquis.[110] And what, O, disciples of split bamboo, braided silk, invisible gut and singing reels, do you suppose was the tackle used on that momentous occasion? A black alder pole, cut on the spot, to "which was attached a discarded bind from the busy spinning wheel, which was then found in almost every dwelling in the State. Fastened to this, by a black linen "gauge" was a small but coarse wired and blunt-pointed hook, with a side bend which we called a "curbed" hook, being as near as we could get to "Kirby."[111] I had caught a small chub with this primitive tackle, and with a boy's cruelty was amusing myself by spinning him through the water, when the tempting bait caught the hungry eye of a magnificent trout, which had probably just turned in from the river to begin the ascent of the stream. With a lightning-like rush he gorged both fish and hook, and then commenced the "tug of war."

Ye Gods!

What a commotion was created in that quiet eddy by the desperate and futile struggles of the noble fish to escape from the cruel hook, and my equally vain and frantic, efforts to lift him from his native element. Finding my strength unequal to

---

[110] The catching of the trout would have been when David was near ten years of age.

[111] The type of fishhook, defined earlier.

the task of lifting him with the awkward and unwieldly pole, I adopted the tactics of un older brother who was over-matched by a big eel; and shouldering my pole, marched inland, dragging my prize ingloriously up the sandy beach, the rotten line giving away just as I got him at a safe distance from the water's edge.

Since that far away day, I have fished the waters of Maine from the Saco to the St. Croix; from the sea to Allegash Lake;[112] have taken the "prismatic beauties" from the streams of Canada and New Brunswick; the crystal brooks of the White Hills of New Hampshire; the Green Mountains of Vermont; from quiet pools and lovely lakelets of the noble North Woods, and the foaming cascades of the "Golden West;"— but the feeling of exultation which filled my breast, as with beating heart I lifted up my glowing prize, has never been excelled.

Hurrying home and proudly displaying my trophy, I well remember my father's remark, that twenty years before, such trout were quite common; but the pickerel were destroying them, and in a short time there would be no trout in any of the streams where the pickerel, could reach. Of course, this statement was gospel to me, and for years I implicitly believed that pickerel were the destruction and bane of trout fishing.

At that time the former fish absolutely swarmed in all waters of the lower Piscataquis and its tributaries. I have taken as many as forty in a single day from a "set net" sixty feet in length, belonging to my father, which I tended for several seasons. When the writer was 13 years of age, his

---

[112] Former spelling of Allagash.

parents removed from the above river, settling down within easy reach of one of the most famous pickerel and trout streams in the State.[113] For ten miles it meanders through a natural meadow, and being totally devoid of current, and filled with eel-grass and lily pads, this formed a sort of pickerel's paradise, and from it I have taken eighty in one day's fishing with a single hook and line. The upper portion was almost equally as good for trout, although there was nothing to prevent the pickerel from going the entire length of the stream, and they were found, although in diminished numbers and of smaller size, wherever a piece of deadwater occurred, throughout the whole stretch of the trout fishing grounds, from which I have caught sixty trout averaging a quarter of a pound apiece as the result of a single day's fishing.

For a dozen years the trout fishing remained almost equally good, the pickerel in the meantime diminishing to less than one-quarter of their original number, owing to the easy accessibility of that portion of the stream by reason of which it was thoroughly fished, especially on wet days during the haying season. During all these years I was not only an enthusiastic trout fisher, but a careful observer of

---

[113] Libbey is referring to the Seboeis Stream, near Howland, Maine, near where his family lived in his youth. Not to be confused with the Seboeis River that branches into the East Branch of the Penobscot near Lookout Mountain. From the latter Seboeis River, there is a Little Seboeis River, which is really a brook in terms of Maine waterways. On a Maine map the designation of a brook, stream, or river may indicate little in relation to the size and flow you may encounter at the locality.

their habits, as well as of those of the pickerel, and my views in regard to the destructiveness of the latter, so far as trout were concerned, had become greatly modified notwithstanding the tenacity with which boyish opinions and prejudices cling to the mind in after life.

The total dissimilarity in their habits and in the character of the waters which they inhabited were among the reasons which contributed to produce this change; but far greater than these was the fact that in all the hundreds, and I might say thousands, of pickerel which I had dressed, not one trout had ever been found. The undigested fish found would be about in proportion of three of their own young to two "chubs" (so called, but really dace).[114] This was a staggerer; for two spring brooks ran directly into the meadow above mentioned, and at the mouths of these, at rare intervals when all conditions were favorable, splendid catches of trout could be made, ranging all the way from one-quarter to three pounds, and some of the latter weight were even occasionally caught among the lily-pads when trolling for pickerel. I reasoned that if the dace could remain in the very haunts of the pickerel in undiminished numbers, when every mess of the pickerel which were dressed proved beyond cavil that the former were being swallowed by thousands, why should they

---

[114] Chubs and dace, from several families of small freshwater fish of the minnow species. Depending on location, one may find the bluntnose minnow, cutlips minnow, Fathead minnow, creek chub, shiners, blacknose dace, longnose dace, and many other types. Dace-type are usually smaller in length, being a few inches; compared to a chub-type of fish that may grow nearer to ten inches, as in the case of a hornyhead chub.

exterminate trout, whose agility not only surpassed both so far as to be beyond comparison, but whose home was in the coldest and swiftest parts of the streams, places abhorred by their foes?

Doubts as to the truth of the assertion heard on every side that the diminution of trout was due to the presence of pickerel having thus arisen in my mind, I have striven by a course of patient observation, extending over a period of more than twenty years, to solve them. The result has been a settled conviction, that *the destruction of trout in their native streams by pickerel is a myth*; and if they are eaten at all it must be in such insignificant numbers as to be totally discarded from among the causes to which we attribute the lessening numbers of trout in certain localities each succeeding year.

This conclusion has been reached, in spite of all my prejudices being in favor of the latter as against the former. Of course, this does not apply to ponds and artificial breeding-places, where the trout have no room or place of escape; for I must not be understood as holding up the idea that a pickerel would not catch a trout if an opportunity presented itself for doing so. I also firmly believe that the ova of trout are never disturbed by them, under any circumstances; and this for two reasons. One is that the pickerel is not a bottom-feeding fish, and, as far as my observations extend, never noticing anything which has not the appearance of life; and although on very dark, cloudy days it can be caught near the bottom, it is necessary, in order to be successful, to let the bait sink, and then raise it suddenly, the fish seizing it as it ascends. Neither does the pickerel move much at night, as anyone who has speared them can testify. The other and stronger reason is the fact that trout always, if possible, select broad and shallow places for their spawning-beds, where the water runs over sand or gravel; and it is no unusual thing to see them depositing their ova in water so shallow that their dorsal fins protrude above the surface. Nothing could be more repugnant to the well-known habits of the pickerel than to remain on such places, and I do not believe the person can be found who ever saw one there. Certainly not the writer.

Immediately after being hatched out, the young trout leave the larger streams and retire up the innumerable runs and rivulets, which always abound on all good trout streams, in many instances passing many roils underground, to reappear in some boiling spring or pool. There they are safe from all enemies, except such as will be hereafter mentioned, and here they remain till they are of a size, which varies according to the character of the water they inhabit. In some little brooks none will be found over four inches in length; in others, which do not appear any larger, they will remain till they are twice that length. Perhaps the greater abundance of food is the cause; at any rate, the facts are as stated.

Having now stated a proposition so much at variance with all preconceived ideas, I wish to fortify it with some facts, to avoid being overwhelmed with the ridicule of unbelievers.

The Little Sebois, to which allusion was made at the beginning of this article, is well known as one of the streams in which the Fish Commissioners have (at two different times, I believe) placed a large supply of young salmon. Twelve miles from its mouth, and three above the place where the salmon were deposited, the stream forks, and at the head of each branch are large lakes. These, as well as the stream throughout its entire length, have been filled with pickerel for over fifty years. On the east branch, eight miles above the forks, is a bog, nearly three miles long. Here the stream is nearly fifty feet in width, and from ten to twenty feet in depth in the driest seasons, when scarcely water enough flows out of it to float an empty canoe. Being eight miles above the nearest settlement (Whitney Ridge),[115] whose inhabitants have plenty of fishing nearer home, the pickerel breed among their favorite lily-pads undisturbed, and there are more of them in that piece of deadwater than in any place I ever saw in my life. From the foot of the bog to the forks it is all rapid water, and in the lower portion of this I caught, two years ago last June,[116] with rod and reel, 104 trout, weighing from 1/4 to 1 ¼ lb. each!

The reason of my great success was undoubtedly due to the fact that a million feet of logs were "hungup" in the stream above, owing to the dry season, and their presence prevented the trout in a measure from ascending; but it shows that the trout were there. They were caught inside of three hours, and from all appearances the catch might have been doubled had one chosen. This stream flows untrammeled by shingle mill or factory. It is too far away for city anglers, and for twenty years the otter and mink have been trapped off it by two of the most skillful trappers in the State. Thus, on this stream, it will be seen, none of the three causes exist, to

---

[115] Whitney Ridge was a small settlement on the shore of what is now named South Branch Lake. The stream here branches into the East and West Branch.

[116] Given this article was published in 1879, and in the fall of 1876 Libbey made his way west, he must be referring to June 1876 or the prior year.

which alone, in my estimation, we are indebted for the destruction of our trout.

At the foot of the bog above mentioned, a dam has been built for driving purposes, the gates of which I found shut, on my first arrival at the place, having been left in that condition by the drivers to save water in case of a "June freshet." As this interfered with some lumbering operations which I designed prosecuting in that vicinity, I hoisted the gate, and launching a canoe into the deadwater above, found that there was nearly two feet of water over the entire bog, which in some places is half a mile in width, and the pickerel had deserted the stream and spread out all over the bog.

Paddling up to where, at low water, a little spring brook came in, I jointed up a trunk rod with which I was provided, together with all the necessary adjuncts, and in less than half an hour caught seven trout, whose weight aggregated ten and one-half pounds. Having no landing-net or companion, I was forced to lift them all in over the side of the canoe by the leader, some of them towing me several rods before they gave up the fight. If anyone has any doubts as to the difficulty of this kind of fishing — standing alone in the centre of an extremely light and "ticklish" birch — a single trial will suffice to convince them of the contrary. Of course, I thought that I had struck a bonanza, and in a very few days revisited the spot for another mess of trout. The water had fallen a foot below the banks, and at the first five casts I succeeded in losing three flies and landing two pickerel. This was exasperating, and removing my leader I substituted a McHarg bait, and without moving from the place where I had fastened my canoe, I caught fifteen pickerel as fast as I could remove the gang from their mouths and recast; sometimes three or four darting for the glittering bait at once. This state of things lasted through the entire season. Sometimes, just before sunrise, or after sunset, I could catch a few noble trout; but the pickerel soon exhausted my stock of flies, and we had to content ourselves with pickerel, save when I could spare time to visit the stream below the dam, where one was always sure of a fair catch of trout. Here, then, is a stream which has been filled with pickerel for more than fifty years, and yet the trout fishing in it will compare favorably with any stream that can be named where pickerel were never known.

But this is far from being the only instance I can name.

Twenty-five years ago, I cut a hole through the ice on Madeceunk Lake[117] and caught through it seven trout and five pickerel. The oldest inhabitant could not then remember when there were no pickerel in Madeceunk Lake; and yet at that time, and for ten years subsequently, the trout fishing, from the outlet to the river (about four miles), was simply superb.

Now the fishing is best represented by an innumerable row of ciphers.[118] And Bangor anglers execrate the pickerel![119]

---

[117] An older spelling for Mattaseunk Lake, just over the county line in Aroostook County, northwest of Mattawamkeag.

[118] The word, cipher, for a person was used to mean someone who had no influence or importance in the world; Libbey showing his disdain for these sportsmen.

[119] In, *Exploring the Maine Woods – The Hardy Family Expedition to the Machias Lakes*, Fannie Eckstorm (certainly

It is singular that the pickerel taste for trout was not developed, after over half a century of quiet existence together, until after the completion of the E. & N. A. R. R.,[120] which sent swarms of fishermen from the city each season on to the banks of the stream, it being only about an hour's drive from Mattawamkeag. Both branches of the Penobscot River are filled with pickerel for many miles, the east, as far as Grand Falls, above which they are not found, and the west, up to and including the lower lakes.[121] Not only is good trout fishing found in the streams flowing into both these branches below the points named, but it is excellent at proper seasons in the branches themselves.

BIG WILSON STREAM

Now let us examine the condition of some famous trout stream, where these scapegoats are not found. A single example will suffice. This shall be the Big Wilson, flowing into Sebec Lake. This magnificent stream, which in any other State would be called a river, flowing from a noble pond through a succession of wooded hills and mountains, fed by

---

not a cipher) did just the opposite and she devoted an entire chapter to the bounty of a pickerel feast.

[120] E. & N. A. R. R, the tracks of the railroad in this region are currently labeled as the Eastern Maine Railroad.

[121] On the East Branch, the Grand Falls referred to is commonly now labeled, Grand Pitch and is just below the Haskell Deadwater. The lower lakes are Ambajejus, Pemadumcook, and North Twin Lakes on the West Branch.

a multitude of sparkling brooks, clear as crystal, seems designed by nature as the very home of the beautiful and agile fish which formerly peopled its waters by thousands.

Where are they now?

Echo answers —*Where*?

It is doubtful if there was a stream within the boundaries of the State, thirty years ago (1840s), where better trout fishing could be found than in the Big Wilson, and certainly there is none of equal size and capacity, and equally free from mills and settlements, where today it is as poor.

And why?

The answer is easy.

Big Wilson Pond is only three miles from the foot of Moosehead Lake, and connected with it by a wagon road. This pond seemed to be the breeding-place of the trout for the entire length of the stream, for the stream was too rough and rocky, apparently, to afford many spawning beds, and all the brooks which flow into it have, owing unfortunately to the mountainous character of the country, falls near their mouths from thirty to eighty feet in height, and above these no trout are found in any of them. Nowhere in that portion of the State were brook trout found so large as in Wilson Pond, and no-where else were they so capricious in their tastes, so shy and so difficult to catch.

Hence a piece of fat pork on a coarse hook had no charms for them, and even the persuasive, wriggling of the angleworm failed to lure many of the wary beauties from their liquid home. Even the skilled angler with all his changes and combinations of artificial flies, would frequently fail for days together to evoke a single rise. But a live minnow attached to two hundred feet of line, towed rapidly through the water by a boat or canoe, was always an effective method to take them; and I regret to say that this unsportsmanlike and disgraceful mode of brook trout fishing has been followed by gentlemen who ought to know better, till the trout in the lake are well-nigh annihilated; and this with the fly and bait fishing for five or six miles below the lake, has been sufficient to destroy the trout fishing in this splendid stream, although there is a long stretch below this (which is) very little fished. This result has been hastened by the obstruction in the brooks mentioned above, and it would be well could some person be found, public-spirited enough, to stock them above the falls, most of them being all that could be desired for trout brooks for miles.

FALLS ALONG LITTLE WILSON STREAM
before merging with Big Wilson Stream
(Editor's Collection)

- - -

But it is not in our own State that the evil effects of over-fishing and unlawful methods of trout taking have reached their full effects, but in the Adirondacks.[122] Take the main road, where if crosses the Indian River, as a central point, and within a circle of ten miles in diameter there are at least thirty ponds, all formerly filled with trout, where now not a one of these beautiful fish can be found. Some of these have been denuded of their trout for years, and some only recently, but all by the same means — persistent fishing, supplemented by the gill-net of professional fishermen to furnish the tables of fashionable hotels at Saratoga. In all these ponds not one pickerel was ever known, but they are now being slily stocked with these fish — not by the guides, who destroyed the trout, but by lovers of legitimate trout fishing, who are exasperated at the infamous mode of their destruction, and who know the utter futility of attempting to restock them with trout. Perhaps in after years, when pickerel shall have become plenty in these ponds, we shall hear that the trout were exterminated by them!

From what one bears of the threatened destruction of trout by pickerel in the Racquette,[123] one would naturally suppose that their introduction there was a very recent matter; but the writer spent part of the autumn and winter of 1866 on that river, and at that time it was filled with pickerel. The amount of trout that were caught after the lakes froze over was simply astounding; they were literally hauled out by horse

---

[122] From Libbey's journal, we know he spent a good deal of time there procuring ship timber.

[123] Sometimes spelled, Raquette, this river cuts through the Adirondacks, originating at Raquette Lake and empties into the St. Lawrence River.

loads. This was about the time Murray's articles were being published in the Atlantic, I believe. These sent hundreds upon hundreds of anglers and pleasure seekers into those sylvan retreats, and to them, and not to the pickerel, is due the diminution in the numbers of trout. But the pickerel of Long Lake and the adjacent waters must not be confounded with those of our own State. They are much more nearly related to the muskalonge of Lake Champlain, the St. Francis River, and other St. Lawrence waters.

A gentleman who owned a large farmland, and also a sawmill, situated on a stream running into Indian River, had on one portion of his land a small pond, about five acres in extent, with a small outlet running into the stream just above the mill. This pond had been totally denuded of trout for some years, and one day, being on a fishing excursion to North River, the thought occurred to him to carry home some pickerel for the purpose of stocking his pond. He therefore took a couple about a foot in length in a large pail with which he happened to be provided, and turned them loose in this pond. By singular good fortune they chanced to be a male and female.

As the outlet, where it left the pond was completely choked up by the debris which had fallen into it, they were unable to get out, and in a few years the pond was fully stocked, but owing to some cause, probably the confined space and want of outlet, they utterly refused to bite any and all kinds of bait. At the end of four years, not having caught a single fish, he furnished himself with a spear, and carrying a light boat into the pond after nightfall, placed a torch in the bow, and succeeded in spearing about twenty, one of which, much larger than any of the rest, and undoubtedly one of the original two placed in the pond, tipped the beam at 15 lbs. The following spring a tremendous freshet swept away the obstructions at the outlet and with them some of the pickerel, one of which he took out of his mill wheel, Weighing 16 lbs. This is sufficient proof that they belong to a different species from ours, as I never saw one at home weighing over 5 1/2 lbs., though I believe they have been caught weighing over 7 lbs. The Maine fish surpasses the former in their edible qualities being whiter, firmer and better tasting. In these respects, the pickerel of Maine is superior to all other inland fishes in the State, save, of course, the trout; nine people out of ten preferring them to white perch. The labor of preparing the perch for the table is also much greater and distasteful to most people.

It is no exaggeration to say that the value of the pickerel in the inland waters of the State surpasses that of all the other fishes combined. By this I mean their commercial value, as food for the people; and for this reason as fast as the country is fully settled, the trout disappear from those localities, and to obtain them one has to go to a distance always requiring time, patience and usually money; and their capture is a matter of pastime and healthful recreation rather than a question of food. But pickerel flourish in ponds and still rivers bordered and surrounded by busy villages and smiling fields. Their flesh is palatable and wholesome the year round, no matter how stagnant and warm are the waters and adverse the surroundings. The reason of the almost impossibility of exterminating them, when nets and spearing are not resorted to, is found in the fact that they distribute themselves over the entire area of the waters they inhabit, never collecting in schools nor congregating at certain points. They also become very wary in waters much fished, sometimes utterly refusing to take bait for weeks at a time. Trout, on the contrary, no matter how large a lake or pond they may be in, invariably as the hot season advances, repair to the mouths of the coolest brooks, or to points where springs break out under water. These places are soon discovered by both anglers and poachers; the former take all they can legitimately, the latter catch them by every means in their power; and the extent to which this is carried on cannot even be guessed at by those who only spend a few days or weeks each season in the enjoyment of trout fishing.

The writer, on a hot day in July, met two young men staggering under a load of trout suspended from a stout pole carried between them on their shoulders, every one of which had been caught at the mouth of a spring brook by means of a grapnel made by tying four hooks together, and suspending it from a short, stiff pole by a line four feet in length; there could not have been less than 100 pounds of them. And I could fill a volume with like instances which have come under my notice.

Next in the order of destruction of the trout come the shingle mills. As far as my observation extends, an ordinary board mill has no bad effect on trout. The stream alluded to, where trout and pickerel fishing abounded for years, had all the time a mill sawing boards only, situated above the best part of the trout fishing grounds. It did not seem to affect them in the least, and it was no unusual thing for the millmen to catch a mess of trout by putting a perforated board across the foot of the apron before shutting down the gate, leaving the trout floundering helplessly on the floor of the apron as the water drained off through the holes in the board. In the course of time a shingle machine was placed in the mill, and in three seasons the trout fishing below it was almost totally destroyed. And this is the way the thing is brought about: It is well known that in all shingle machines in use at the present day the bolt either descends vertically upon the saw; or if moving horizontally, it is placed on end, so that in either case the saw strikes its side, cutting a chip out the whole length of the bolt.[124] This is technically termed "long sawdust," and being whirled into eddies below the mill, collects into rolls and bunches sometimes as large as a ten-gallon keg. As the thirsty sun drinks up the waters, the mill has to be shut down; these bundles become water-logged and sink to the bottom. In October and November when the trout have fairly deposited their ova, the fall rains come on, the masses of sawdust, too heavy to float and too light to remain fixed to the bottom, go rolling down the stream. The greatest ingenuity could not devise a more potent engine of destruction. As they sweep over the spawning beds the ova is caught up by a thousand points which bristle in every direction, and carried to the still, deep water below, where is devoured by swarms of hungry dace, perch and cat-fish (horn pouts).

Lastly in the order of destructive forces come the mink, muskrat and otter, though perhaps if the whole country were taken into consideration their depredations would be found to exceed either of the others. Their evil effects are in inverse proportion to the others, being greatest where the others are least. People who have not actually observed them can form

---

[124] The 'bolt' refers to the piece of timber being milled. Bole was the main stem, bolt a shorter stem.

no adequate conception of the havoc a family of otters will work in a trout stream, and above all, in a pond upon a spawning bed. The writer once watched a family of five, which were fishing in a pond between Monson and Moosehead Lake. The rapidity with which they caught and devoured the fish was amazing, and as they were obliged to come to the surface to swallow them, I could see each one caught. This infringement on the rights of man made my blood boil, and the driving of a bullet through the head of one of them, which I succeeded in doing, is still considered one of the most satisfactory performances of my life.

On another occasion, when traveling along the bank of a stream in New Brunswick during a prolonged drought when scarcely a drop of water ran in the stream, I discovered in a deep pool, several rods in extent, at least a hundred trout from six inches to a foot and a half in length. The next day on repassing the same place, only three remained, one of these, the very largest, so scarred by the teeth of otter that he must have died. The bank afforded abundant evidence of their destructive visit. Mink confine their depredations chiefly to the smaller brooks and rivulets, where they work almost equal destruction among the small trout.

A pleasant writer in a recent number of the *Portland Transcript* expressed a fear that trout would eventually be annihilated! His fears are undoubtedly only too well founded as far as Moosehead and the Rangeley Lakes are concerned, for where two trout are caught to one hatched it does not require a very brilliant intellect to forecast the ultimate result. But to anyone familiar with the vast water resources of Maine, enveloped and surrounded as they are by an almost pathless forest, such a result will appear impossible as long as anything like the present conditions exist. Take for example the tract bounded on the east and west by the St. Croix and Penobscot Rivers, and on the north and south by the E. & N. A. R. R. and the old Air Line Stage Road — a tract about one hundred miles square.[125] Here one might fish for a lifetime, finding no lack of sport, and still one could not be considered as even having entered the outskirts of Maine's vast wilderness.

NET RESULTS
(From, *Thomas S. Steele's Maine Adventures*
Two-book Collection.
Burnt Jacket Publishing, 2021.)

---

[125] The Airline Road that was the route of a stagecoach. The road is still named as such today.

AN EAST BRANCH TRIP

IN the final part of the 1879 article, Libbey gives the readers from across the United States a tour of the river. In that year, very few citizens would have had the opportunity to see this part of the country he describes. Certainly, before Libbey penned this essay, Thoreau wrote of the region and his canoe trip, as did Hubbard and Steele. But here, Libbey is taking the more difficult way, against the current.

- - -

LET us take a flying trip in imagination into the heart of this almost *terra incognita*, choosing Nicketou,[126] at the junction of the two branches of the Penobscot, as our starting point, and the East Branch as our route. With a good guide and canoe, a week's not over hard work will bring us to Grand Lake, passing on our way the Wissattiquoik, swiftest of streams, tumbling from off Mt. Katahdin from the west, its pellucid waters filled with trout, and its numerous ponds teeming with both brook trout and "lakers."[127] Not far above it, on the eastern side, rolls in the Big Sebois, a noble stream, whose numberless tributaries and magnificent lakes would

---

[126] Libbey is referring to Nickatou Island for this starting point, at the intersection of the West Branch, East Branch, and Main Branch of the Penobscot River.

[127] Grand Lake noted here refers to what is now labeled, Grand Lake Matagamon. Originally, Matangamook Lake.

require a whole season to explore.[128] Just below Grand Lake is the mouth of "Phil. Fish Brook," which, I presume, is the one alluded to by another correspondent of the *Transcript* as "Bill Fish Brook."[129] It was named after a Bangor lumberman; equally well known for his skill in river driving and his reckless habits. Its waters are more nearly transparent than any the writer ever saw. So clear are they that, looking down into them from a canoe, one seems to be suspended in air. At its head are a pair of beautiful twin ponds, from which two well-known Bangor lumbermen once took nearly three hundred trout through the ice one rainy day in March.

The dam at the outlet of Grand Lake, just above the brook's mouth, is one of the greatest places for trout in the State, as it is shut down till the last drive arrives at the foot of the lake, no trout are able to get above it, and they swarm in the deep holes at the foot of the aprons by the hundreds. The writer has seen a pork barrel nearly filled with those caught by the cook of a crew which had arrived first at the

---

[128] The river names noted may cause confusion. On the edition of the editor's Maine Gazetteer, the river in this area has been labelled as Seboeis. On Hubbard's 1899 map it is Seboois. The Gazetteer used the same spelling, Seboeis, also for a different river near Howland and the lake from which it flows. The Native American names from which these derived were based on locality, and they did not mean the same, nor were they spelled the same. A modern map-maker misinterpreted the original spellings.

[129] Libbey referred to this brook with the name known at the time, as Phil. Fish Brook. On the editor's edition of the Maine Gazetteer, the brook and the pond have been renamed Bill Fish, the lumberman long since forgotten and likely another case of mistaken identity on a map.

dam and was waiting for the "hind drives."[130] Grand Lake, four miles long, and nearly as broad, is a lovely sheet of water, and was formerly peopled by a singular species of the genus *Salmo*, called togue. It bore not the faintest resemblance to any variety of the trout family, with the exception of having the adipose second dorsal fin. It very nearly resembles a sucker, or mullet, in the squareness and coarseness of its outline, being broadest and deepest just at the base of the gill covers, tapering from thence to the tail, which was narrower and more forked than even a "laker's." Black on its back, dark gray on its sides, grayish-white underneath, with a very few large black spots on each side, just back of the pectoral fins. But its most remarkable characteristic was a large callosity on the end of the lower jaw, perfectly round, and flat in front, being larger across in a full-sized fish than a ten-cent piece. It was a very sluggish fish, without the slightest approach to gameness; its flesh was white, of a muddy and rather disagreeable taste, and smelled so strongly when cooking as to be almost nauseating.

When the "cut" was made,[131] connecting the St. John waters with those of the Penobscot, the lakers, almost exactly resembling those of Moosehead and St. Croix Lakes, came down into Grand Lake, and the togue began to slowly disappear. At present I do not believe one can be found in the

---

[130] Hind Drives, meaning the last to come down the rivers. Each drive had a front and rear. The last drives were called the hind drives, or the rear.

[131] Referring to the Telos Cut, a canal dug by lumbermen to route the headwaters south into the West Branch of the Penobscot.

lake, nor any like them in the State. They have been caught weighing as high as forty pounds. At the northwestern extremity of Grand Lake, Trout Brook comes in — about twenty-five miles long, with splendid trout fishing throughout its entire length. On this stream and its tributaries there are perhaps twenty ponds, all, I believe, containing trout; and in one of them — not more than four acres in extent, with no inlet, and an outlet not more than a yard wide — a laker was caught weighing sixteen pounds. [By laker is meant the *Salmo confinis*.[132]] A thoroughfare four miles in length connects Grand with Second Lake. In this thoroughfare, for a short time during each season, the trout fishing is superb; and such trout! running from one and a half to four pounds.

Second Lake is three miles long, and a few rods above it is the mouth of Webster Brook, formerly a small tributary of the East Branch; but now, owing to the admission of the Allegash waters through the "cut," three times as large as the main stream. Ten miles of the roughest kind of water up this stream brings us to Webster Lake. Here, one winter, when moose hunting, the writer once caught a mess of trout out of an "air-hole" near the inlet, which is, he thinks, almost unprecedented. At the head of this lake is the "cut," three-fourths of a mile in length, which brings us to what was formerly the head of the Telos Lake, but is now called its foot, its waters being turned back by a massive dam at the foot of Chamberlain Lake. Telos Lake is five miles long, and has at least one magnificent trout stream.

---

[132] *Salmo confinis*, originally described by DeKay in 1842, belonging to the family *Salmonidae* and subfamily *Salmoninae*.

A short thoroughfare brings us to Round Pond, two miles in length, and a favorite spot in winter for the hardy lumbermen to catch lakers through the ice.

Another short thoroughfare, and we are fairly launched on Chamberlain Lake, a noble expanse of water twelve miles in length; or, if reckoned from the extremities of its "arms," eighteen.

We have now reached the heart of the Great Maine Wilderness. Far below us to the southward, blue in the distance, loom up the rugged peaks of old Katahdin; around us, dark, unbroken, almost illimitable, stretches the primeval forest. In its dusky shadows roam the fleet caribou and the lordly moose, the latter, alas! now few and far between.[133] No costly hotels invite the fastidious angler to repose his weary limbs after the fatigues of the day, or tempt his palate with tables covered with all the delicacies of the season. A large lumberman's farm on the eastern shore has one rude dwelling, surrounded by numerous barns, where one is welcome to the rough fare of the lumber camps.[134] But here the trout sport in all their native freedom; and here they will continue to sport long after the fishing at Moosehead and Rangeley Lakes shall be only a pleasant memory to anglers who have laid aside the rod for the cane.

---

[133] Libbey would be pleased to find that the moose now thrive in the north Maine woods. The caribou, however, are no longer, they were not even able to survive an experiment in the 1980s to repatriate them to Maine.

[134] Referring to Chamberlain Farm, covered more fully in the writings by Steele, Hubbard, and Eckstorm. These titles can be found at the end of this book.

From here three routes are open for our return. We can go to the northern extremity of the lake, and down the Allegash and St. John to Fredericton; or to the west, across Mud Pond Carry into the West Branch, and down that to the point of departure; or up it to the Northwest Carry, and across that to Moosehead Lake.

Penobscot.
San Francisco, March 27, 1879.

- - -

The route David Libbey described is opposite of the direction most explorers took during their travels in this region. He, being a river-driver, probably had poled his way against the river's current many times. The more common direction for this trip was to take a steamer from Greenville to Northeast Carry. From there, the canoe would be portaged to the West Branch of the Penobscot.

TROUTING AROUND LAKE MEGANTIC

EVEN though Libbey was back in Maine, he didn't always stay close to home. In this 1882 article, he writes of his fishing trip to Lake Megantic, near the Maine border west of Jackman, Maine. This trip occurred sometime between 1880 and 1882.[135] The lumberman, turned story-teller, is apparent in this entertaining essay of adventure. The trip was taken for the sheer joy of being again on the water, for why else would one paddle eight miles with a crooked oar?

I HAD made excursions to various trout streams in different directions and everywhere found the number of trout disproportionate to the swarms of black flies that I was nearly discouraged and wholly disgusted, albeit my desire for a good day's fishing grew stronger at every failure. In this emergency I applied to "Old Paradis"— everybody knows Old Paradis. As a whisky-drinker, fiddler and trout-fisher he stands at the head. As a carpenter, upholsterer and plasterer he is above the average; his stories are inexhaustible, and his garrulity illimitable. Now, I grieve to say that a long and bitter experience has taught me to totally disregard all stories of wonderful trout-fishing in any and all places. I listen with real or feigned interest, expressing pleasure or wonder according to the size of the story, and then if I wish to go fishing, I apply the test:

Did he know of any good trout pond that could be reached that day?

"Yes, indeed. Eight miles up the lake, on the west shore, a little brook comes in; follow that up for a mile and a half and you come to Grosbois Pond."

He had visited it half a dozen times, and never failed of a good catch; then came the test question:

Would he go with me?

"Certainly." *If I* could furnish the tackle, as his was all at home.

This I readily agreed to do.

The only boat obtainable was a light cedar skiff, owned by Major McAulay of the Prince of Wales Hotel, which had been bought the spring before for a regatta on the Queen's birthday, and, distancing all competitors, had been named Flash.[136]

We resurrected it from under a pile of rubbish in the boat house where it had lain all winter, and then found it to be just a wreck, with gaping seams, seats torn from their fastenings, and streaks sun-cracked through and through.

---

[136] Regattas are routinely held during celebrations in Canada, a tradition dating back to the early 1800s.

- - -

CANADIAN HOTELS.

The following hotels are located in the vicinity of Lake Megantic. Prices are from $1.00 to $3.00 per day : —

AGNES (P. Q.).

Chaudière House, M. Morrison, prop.
Prince of Wales Hotel, M. B. McAuley, prop.
Victoria Hotel, A. W. Pope, prop.
American House, Jeremiah Ham, prop.
Hotel Megantic, Henry Pouton, prop.
Nantais Hotel, I. Moquin, prop.

Advertisement for Canadian Hotels.

From, *Sportsmen's and Tourists' Guide Book to the Dead River Region of Maine* (1884).

Notice the proprietor's name listed for the Prince of Wales Hotel is Major McAuley.

- - -

However, it was still early morning, and as either of us were fully competent to build an entire boat, we went to work with a will, and by 8 o'clock had it ready to launch. Then we hunted up two frightfully deformed oars of entirely different pattern, weight and length, each one of which crooked three ways, and I could feel in anticipation the blisters which would adorn my hands at the end of the eight-mile row. A light breeze milled the surface of old Megantic as we rowed leisurely up it.

The grand old forest looked very pleasant on either side, the bright green of the birches and maples just coming into full leaf, contrasting beautifully with the dark verdure of the evergreen spruce and fir. A two hours' pull brought us to the mouth of the brook, and with hands burning from their contact with the infernal implement of torture, which ought to have been an oar, I shouldered axe and fishing rod and we started up the brook. I found it filled with trout, but saw none over six inches in length, but have no doubt that the fisherman "for count" could have gone into the hundreds.

Arriving at the pond I was surprised to find a heavy dam at the foot, and then I learned that the name of the pond did not arise from the size of the timber with which it was surrounded, as I had supposed, but that a Frenchman of that name built the dam with the intention of building a sawmill, but his funds giving out after damming the brook, he done the same thing to the location and left.[137]

The pond is a third of a mile in length, and half that distance across, and is nothing in fact but a huge spring with scarcely any inlets, the water clear as crystal, nowhere more than four or five feet in depth, and the bottom a brown mud of unfathomable depth. Our first care was to build a raft, for which purpose we had brought the axe. Plenty of dry cedar logs were lying close to the bank, and while cutting them into suitable lengths, my ears were regaled with a noble song from a Rose-breasted Grosbeak hidden in the dense foliage of a huge sugar maple a few rods away

---

[137] Grosbois, has among its English interpretations, that of heavy timber.

We soon had timber enough for our raft, and as I stooped to pick up the last log, a flood of melody from a cedar thicket, whose top was just illuminated by the red rays of the setting sun, caused me to suddenly pause, all my faculties engrossed in the one sense of hearing. It was the song of the hermit thrush, a song forever associated in my mind with trout fishing in my boyhood's happy days, when free from care I wandered barefoot among the dripping alders down the brook, and heard the swamp robin's song on every hand, liquid and clear. The melodious and flute-like notes floated out on the calm air of that beautiful June evening, and as I listened, my surroundings faded from my view, and I stood in the deserts of Nevada and saw again the tears in the eyes of a fellow countryman, who told me there that one of the greatest desires of his life was to hear again the song of the hermit thrush. I pulled myself back into the present with a wrench, and saw Paradis looking at me half in amazement, half in contempt. I knew that the poor wretch thought I was afraid of bears. He had not even heard the song.

Launching our raft, we made our way slowly to the center of the pond. There was not a particle of vegetation to be seen, and the bottom could be discerned for rods in every direction, and the outlook was far from promising. Paradis declared that the bottom was covered in many places the previous summer with eel-grass and lily pads, and its total disappearance confounded him. He insisted on fishing with a fly; but knowing that it was not according to the habits of trout to rise in shallow water unprotected by vegetation, and in clear weather, I baited carefully with worms, and being provided with a thirteen-foot rod, I unreeled as much line as I could conveniently handle and by dint of making long casts and letting my bait slowly settle, I succeeded in landing half a dozen nice trout in the very finest color and condition, their sides glistening like silver as they were taken from the water.

Our stopping place for the night was to be at Myer's Mill, on the shore of the lake, half a mile above the mouth of our brook, so that we had to "pull for the shore" in order to get to land before total darkness set in.

The next morning, we were on the ground in good season. The sun rose bright and cloudless and the prospect for a successful day's fishing looked dubious; but by adopting the tactics of the previous evening I got now and then a trout, the intervals growing longer and longer as the sun climbed higher in the heavens. Paradis still clung to his fly, although he had caught only two trout. I was about to propose an adjournment, when, happening to cast my eyes to the west, I saw a heavy bank of clouds rapidly climbing toward the zenith. In ten minutes, the sun was hidden, the thermometer went down with a rush, and a hail-storm seemed imminent.

I was about to flee for shelter, when I heard a musical splash and gurgle behind me. Turning my head, I saw Paradis's rod in the form of an arc, and I stood with suspended rod, watching the struggle. He soon had him landed, and making another cast, his fly was again seized the instant it touched the water.

Then I reeled in my line, and with fingers that trembled with eagerness began to tie on a cast of flies. Before I could make a cast, Paradis had landed five trout. Then the rain came down, so cold that it was almost snow, and my fingers soon became so numb that I could scarcely handle my fish; but, for an hour, how the trout did rise! Then the clouds rolled away, the sun came out in cloudless splendor, the fish stopped rising, and we decided that we had enough.

Wet and chilly, we made our way to our boat. The rowing exercise soon warmed us up; but our pile, of trout, so far from hindering us, seemed to help us along wonderfully. I reached the hotel tired and hungry, but well pleased with my trip to Grosbois Pond.

- Penobscot.

- - -

Editor note: Imagine, a fishing expedition in which you first spend the morning repairing a dilapidated skiff, then you row yourself eight miles – using warped, mis-sized oars – to a brook of a small size, which the skiff you labored over is too large a craft for the depth, requiring you then to set out on foot. When you finally arrive at the pond – a mere spring-fed, unvegetated mud hole – you are not disappointed, but rather you take your axe and commence to build a raft. All in a day's adventure with the likes of David Libbey.

COW MOOSE
(Editor's Collection)

MOOSE TRANSPORT

IN his later years, David Libbey continued to submit wildlife and nature stories to magazines. At the age of 73, Libbey wrote this article about deer, partridges, a moose, and a murderous wife, for which he adds (*it seems*) a bit of humor to show how Bill, in the end, got his due.[138]

FOR the last few years, it has become almost a fad among self-styled sportsmen, who know nothing whatever of the subject; as well as a few guides, who ought to know better, to account for the scarcity of deer in any locality, by their having starved to death the preceding winter. Such a claim is an insult to nature. Do the musk ox and reindeer of the frozen and desolate region within the Arctic circle perish of hunger? Do the ptarmigan, who burrow in the deep snows of the far north become embedded under the crust? Certainly not. If

---

[138] *Deer Do Not Starve, and Partridges Do Not Become Imbedded Under the Crust. Calf Moose Tries Walking on Snowshoes*, Maine Woods, Vol. XXIII, No. 24., Jan. 25, 1901.

they did, they would surely become exterminated; but nature never makes mistakes. When she places the wild denizens of the forests in their respective localities, she adapts them perfectly to the conditions under which they are to live, and there is no more danger of the deer in the woods of Maine, dying of starvation, than there is of the antelope, on the bare and arid plains of the southwest perishing of heat and drouth.

I have spent more than fifty winters in the woods and during that time have built and occupied camps in Maine, New Hampshire, Vermont, New York, New Brunswick, and the Province of Quebec; I have been among deer in March, with six feet of snow on the ground, when one could walk up to them and pat them as one would cattle in a barn yard; but I never yet found a deer starved to death, or in a state of starvation. Indeed, the poorest deer that I ever saw were killed in the fall. I have shot three old bucks at widely different times, two in November and one in December so emaciated that they were totally unfit for food, and had to be left where they fell. It is self-evident that if deer starve now, they must always have starved; for no one will have the assurance to claim that our winters are increasing in severity.

But do the veteran hunters of this state, who have passed the most of their lives among the big game, make any such statements? Did ever anyone hear Jock Darling, Alex McLain, Andrew Douglass, Hiram Leonard, Silas McPheters or any other experienced and intelligent hunter say that deer ever died of starvation? Not much! Deer never die of starvation till they die of old age.

The common belief, that partridges become buried under a crust is, in my opinion equally erroneous. Having never found one thus imprisoned, nor seen where one was dug out by foxes or any other animal, I decline to believe that they are ever destroyed in that manner. My memory goes back to the time when one man, with no dog, shot twenty partridges (ruffed grouse) in one day. Were there no crusts in those days? Better come *up to scratch* my fellow sportsmen and frankly admit the truth, that the scarcity of partridges is wholly owing to the multiplicity of hunters, breech loaders and dogs.

Right in line with the above is the notion, universally believed, that pickerel destroy trout. Forty years ago I cut a hole through the ice at the head of Madeceunk Lake, and took therefrom, seven pickerel and five trout.[139] Twenty years after, when the E. & N. A. R. R.[140] brought crowds of down-river anglers who depleted the stream from its mouth to its source, we were gravely informed in the papers of that day, that the pickerel had ruined the trout fishing in the Madeceunk. When the black bass craze swept over the state, the prediction was freely made that they would destroy the trout in all waters that they could reach and when nothing of the kind took place, we were treated to the remarkably sensible and logical deduction, that although pickerel could easily get away with trout, and bass were fully competent to destroy the pickerel, yet they could not catch the trout. Verily the old man of many wives who declared that though you brayed a fool in a mortar, yet would his folly not depart from him, knew what he was talking about.[141]

---

[139] See essay in this volume, "Do Pickerel Destroy Trout."
[140] European and North American Railroad.
[141] A statement referencing, Proverbs 27:22.

- - -

IT wouldn't be fitting for *Penobscot* to not have a good moose story – I'm sure he had many – but the following tale describing a novel way a moose traveled over the snow is especially entertaining. Most of the information he relays is now widely known, but at the time, the habits of the moose and descriptions of the animal may have been more myth than fact, errors he stood to correct.

The following is from the same prior article. The person he names as 'Winchester,' was another contributor to the same magazine.

- - -

I was delighted with Winchester's story of the intelligent cow moose and her tractable calf, because I have long known a story which vividly illustrates those traits, but have never dared to tell it for fear that I would not be believed, for if there is anything that I pride myself on, above my skill as a still hunter, it is my entire and absolute truthfulness. Old age is gradually incapacitating me for the exercising of the first accomplishment, and sometimes I have a frightful suspicion that it is weakening my hold on the last, which grieves me beyond measure, for when I was a kid at my father's knee, he taught me impressively that the meanest thing in the form of humanity that encumbered the face of the earth was a thief, and after him came the liar, and I actually came to believe that preposterously ridiculous and old-fashioned doctrine.

But the story.

- - -

AWAY back in 1860, Josi, Bill, and myself were hunting on snowshoes between Telos and Sourdnahunk Lakes, filling a contract for three tons of moose meat.[142] We had found a yard containing a 3-year old and an old cow and calf, and had killed the two former but spared the calf, at Bill's earnest solicitation, as he said it had a mischievous gleam in its eye that reminded him of his best girl in Chepacket, (he was a Rhode Islander.)[143] It was such an unheard of thing for him to indulge in sentiment, that from pure astonishment we refrained from killing it. Poor Bill! He was always doing the wrong thing; as witness his last exploit. He gave his temporary wife a fearful thrashing to keep her quiet while he indulged in a drunken sleep, of which condition she took advantage to blow his brains out with his double-barreled

---

[142] At the time, being the 1850s and 1860s this was common practice for market hunting.

[143] Chepachet is a village in the town of Glocester in the state of Rhode Island.

shotgun. However, this happened afterwards, as you may have guessed.

Well, we stuck up our snowshoes in the snow near the head of the cow moose, the calf meanwhile not showing any disposition to leave, and went over a sharp knoll a few rods away to where we had killed the 3-year-old. After dressing it and burying the quarters in the snow, we returned to the first moose, to repeat the operation there. Things did not look quite normal.

"Where is the calf?" I asked.

"Where are our snowshoes?" cried Josi.

"Calf? Snowshoes?" said Bill, looking with an air of stupefaction, from one of us to the other.

"You have hit it," I cried. "Calf and snowshoes have evidently gone off together." My own were left where I had left them, only two pairs being taken, and hastily putting them on, I started on the trail. I did not have far to go. Over the edge of the ridge, on a little intervale, where a mountain brook was gurgling between its banks, I saw him just ahead of me, so deeply engaged in solving the problem of locomotion on snowshoes that he never saw me. The intelligent little fellow had discovered that his ordinary mode of traveling was not adapted to snowshoeing, and he was studying up a new gait.

It was soon evident that he had a firm grasp on the situation, for he suddenly started at a pacing gait, swinging one side at a time. I started for him at once, and my sudden rush and shout upset the nice poise of his newly acquired knowledge. He struck a square trot, brought his hind snowshoe onto his forward one, pitched forward on his nose and rolled over on his back. As this was the best position for taking off his snowshoes, I proceeded to divest him of them with neatness and dispatch.

The little wretch, instead of being grateful to me for sparing his life, actually tried to kick me while I was doing it, and I shall never forget the look of deep reproach in his eyes as I tucked the snowshoes under my arm preparatory to rejoining my companions. We dressed the moose and started for camp, Josi moralizing the whole way on the folly of sparing anything, because it had eyes like a frisky girl!

I have already taken up so much space that I can merely glance at "Buck-skin Sam's" feat of killing five bears in six minutes. I would suggest, however, that the next time he meets a swarm of bears instead of taking out his watch to time the combat, he should shove a few more cartridges into the magazine of his rifle. I would also note that the fact that bears remain out of their dens till the snow gets too deep for them to wallow through is entirely unknown to bear hunters of this state.

- Penobscot

- - - -

It appears that David Libbey had some questions about Buckskin Sam's stories. The six-minute bear story Libbey referenced was told by Sam to have taken place near Byron, Maine on West Mountain.

BUCKSKIN SAM – SAMUEL H. NOBLE

(From, *Life and Adventures of Buckskin Sam*, 1900.)

IT IS OCTOBER

DAVID LIBBEY was a river-driver, hunter, fisherman, trapper, traveler, inventor, digger of knees, farmer, lumberman, writer, reader, singer, lumber-camp cook, stationery store clerk, and now a poet. If Kipling paid homage to the Red Gods, here Libbey shows his love for the Open Season. From his own letters, and hints Eckstorm gave about the journal notes, we know he wrote other verses, but none but this one has been found by the editor. This one belongs on the wall at deer camp.

IT IS OCTOBER![144]

WHEN frosty nights succeed the sunny days,
And hunters range the gleaming forests over,
And round the mountains hangs a purple haze,
    It is October.

When anglers lay their rods and baskets by,
Pack leaders, reels and flies with faces sober,
And lock them up, with many a wistful sigh,
    It is October.

When partridges steal softly from the woods
At eve, to seek their food amid the clover.
And in the sunny glades the woodcock broods,
    It is October.

---

[144] Aside from in his journal, the poem appeared in *Forest And Stream*, issue Vol. 19, No. 13, 1882.

When timid does put on their coats of blue,
And antlered bucks forsake the thicket cover,
To roam, with listening ears, the forests through,
    It is October.

When forests burn in crimson, gold and dun,
And hounds with mellow throats track woodlands
over,
When round the lakes is heard the booming gun,
    It is October.

signed, *Penobscot*

BUCK AND DOE DEER

(From, *In the Wilds of The Aroostook Woods – Charles C.
West*, 1892.)

THE FINAL HUNT

DAVID LIBBEY lived a peaceful, quiet, happy life, full of moderate enjoyments. He left it without thought of parting; death was like going into another room. It was tragedy, but such tragedy as he might have elected for himself. With his son, a grandson, and his valued friend, Mr. E. A. Weatherbee, he was at a camp in the town of Chester deer-hunting. On the morning of December 6, 1904, each one went out alone to track deer.

"And if anything happens to one of us," said he, "let the signals be thus and thus." In the evening he did not return and he had not signaled.

In the morning they found him. A light snow, not obliterating his track, had spread a thin blanket over him, and he lay as one asleep, his rifle carefully protected by his coat. There had been no struggle, no consciousness of the bullet which brought him death. He lay close beside a logging-road where the track of the deer he was following crossed it. As he came up, a boy, standing in the road ahead of him, had heard the frozen sprouts rattle, and, just as Libbey was emerging from the woods, had fired with deadly haste. Then he saw what he had done; and having looked, he ran away. In two steps more David Libbey would have been in plain sight, in four steps he would have been in the road itself. What is the fate that ordains tragedy by such narrow margins?

And yet it was not an unkindly doom which left him to round out his full six and seventy in the perfect possession of his powers of mind and body, still keen in the chase, with his eyes bent forward and something yet to desire, and then translated him without pain, or forecast of evil, or the dread of dying. For men who have lived their best, bravely, sincerely, fate commonly seems to devise an exit both honorable and dramatically fit. This was perhaps the foremost hunter in the state; and he died still at his hunting, not having realized that at six and seventy a man is beginning to age and to lose his grip on manly pastimes.

Personally, David Libbey was a small, quiet man of a cheery disposition who won friends on sight. He was alert, observant, receptive rather than expansive. Says Mr. Weatherbee, who knew him as well as any one: "He was first of all a truthful man and thoroughly honest in every way, no sham or pretense about him. He was not only honest as we commonly use the term, but honorable, under no circumstances repeating anything told in confidence, nor saying nor doing anything that a high-minded gentleman should not do. He was the most patient man and the most cheerful under difficulties that I ever knew. He was so much a philosopher that annoyances did not vex him in the least degree, while difficulties only made him determined. He was loyal to his friends, and his intercourse with them put them at their best. I doubt if ever, in his own mind even, he saw any fault in any of his relatives or immediate friends. He had the most childlike faith in human nature; the honesty and the truthfulness of others he never appeared to doubt, judging them by himself; but woe to the one who deceived him! I think he hated a liar as much as he hated a thief. He was one of the very few men who could be convinced at the moment of argument, and he seemed as contented to have you correct as to be correct himself. There never seemed to be any personal element in his arguments. This openness to change caused him to want the latest improvements in tools, and firearms. Nothing was too modern for him."

His son speaks of his moderation in all things, both sport and appetite, an abstemious man who used the gifts of life so well that he never lost his taste for them. Thousands of times he had lighted his campfire and put the trout or venison on to cook over his little hunter's blaze, and yet on the last day, as on the first, it was still a keen delight to him to do it, and the trout still tasted good.

The very last day of his life he was following the deer with all the zest of youth — "to get a handsome buck's head for Allie."

"Bolts and bars were a thing unknown to him," writes this daughter; "he never locked the doors of his house at night, the latchstring always out the same as in camp. He had the true spirit of hospitality, sharing alike the humble meal in the log cabin, the precious bit from his soldier's box from home, the supper cooked by his own hands under the hemlocks in camp, or when at his own fireside. He was utterly fearless as to harm coming to him, and he never harmed a human being. His faith was remarkable, as was the way that he saw and acknowledged good traits in men who had wronged him, and he spared not his praise of them with his voice nor pen."

And again:

"In his home life every day was characterized by a childlike faith in human nature, a reverence for all things good and beautiful, a devotion of nearly fifty years to his faithful companion and an unwavering love for his children. He served a long and faithful apprenticeship to his duty, never hesitating at the crossroads where duty and inclination each stood waiting.

"The gulf-stream of youth flowed steadily through his seventy-six years and no one would dream, to hear him singing cheerily at his daily tasks, that he was often weary in body and harassed in mind, — or, to use his own good words,

'Tired in body but refreshed in spirit, at peace with all the world and in my heart a feeling that life is really worth living.'"

"I can see him best," writes his daughter, "hunting in the woods, or beside the fire in camp at night, or sometimes a vision of my Dad comes to me, sitting on a green bank fishing and softly humming that strain from "Elijah" with which the last book he was reading had opened:

He watching over Israel slumbereth not

nor sleeps."[145]

A QUIET CAMPING SPOT

(From, *The Northern*, 1921.)

---

[145] King James Bible from Psalms 121:4, "Behold, he that keepeth Israel shall neither slumber nor sleep."

When our youthful days are ended, we will
  cease from winter toil,
And each one through the summer warm will till
  the virgin soil;
We've enough to eat, to drink, to wear, content
  through life to go,
Then we'll tell our wild adventures o'er, and no
  more a lumbering go;
And no more a lumbering go, so no more a
  lumbering go,
O! we'll tell our wild adventures o'er, so no
  more a lumbering go.

from, The Logger's Boast

AN UNTIMELY END

David Stone Libbey
August, 22, 1828 - December 6, 1904
Age 76

THE following notice appeared in the *Forest and Stream* issue of December 24, 1904. Note, the magazine had spelled his name as *Libby*. After so many years his signing his letters, *Penobscot*, they were either unaccustomed to how he himself spelled his family name, or the notice was submitted by someone who spelled the name Libby.

David S. Libby

Of fatalities resulting from the reckless use of firearms and shooting accidents during the past autumn, one of the saddest cases was that of David S. Libby, of Newport, Me., who was killed by a hunter who presumably mistook the man for a deer. Mr. Libby was camping with a son and grandson and others in a camp built by him about seven miles from Lincoln, a district in which he had hunted for many years. He left camp one morning to hunt, and did not return that night. The men in camp fired signal guns all night, and in the morning made a search for their missing companion. The lifeless body was found in some bushes just off from a woods road. A bullet hole through the breast showed that death must have been instantaneous. The story told by the snow showed that Mr. Libby had been about to step out into the road, and that two steps more would have taken him into plain view of the person who had fired the shot, and who at the time, as the snow also recorded, had stood not more than thirty feet away. After the firing the shooter had run to the spot where his victim had fallen, and then had taken flight. This heartless conduct aroused the greatest indignation, and it is said that while a conviction for shooting a human being by mistake for game has never yet been had in Maine, the public feeling in this case is so intense that it would go hard with the perpetrator of the deed could his identity be discovered.

Mr. Libby, who had reached the age of 76, was one of the most experienced and most skillful hunters in Maine; and one whose vast information in the field of woodcraft was most highly respected by all who were conversant with it. As a writer over the signature of *Penobscot*, he was for many years a valued contributor to the columns of this journal. There was perhaps in the entire State of Maine no one who in the wilderness was more cautious than he, more circumspect to avoid danger, or better fitted to take care of himself in any ordinary emergency. It is the mockery of fate that such a man should fall victim to that criminal heedlessness against which no experience, no provident forethought, nothing can avail to secure protection.

And this was published in the **Maine Woods**.

- - -

Mystery Surrounding Libby's Death Solved
Maine Woods: Vol. 27, Issue 20 - December 23, 1904

THE mystery surrounding the death of David Libby of Newport who was found dead Dec. 7 at Chester, where he was on a hunting trip, was cleared up last Friday when Herbert E. Griffin, aged 17 years, upon being arrested by Sheriff Gilman and Deputy Stevens, confessed that he did the shooting, having mistaken Libby for a deer.

The boy was arraigned before Trial Justice Weatherbee and was bound over to the February criminal term of the Supreme Court in the sum of $1,000. His father, a prosperous farmer, and a brother furnished bonds.

The penalty fixed by a recently enacted statute law is a fine of not more than $1,000 or imprisonment for not more than ten years, when the shooting is committed carelessly or negligently. Only one or two cases under this law have been held for the grand jury.

The boy's desire in his fright at finding he had shot his companion was to escape and avoid detection. At first he denied all knowledge but while showing the officers the route over which he and Libby had passed he broke down and related the story of the accident. The officers previously had learned that Griffin was seen to leave the woods in a hurried manner about the time of the shooting and empty shells similar to those used in his rifle were found near the body. — Bangor News

WEST BRANCH PENOBSCOT RIVER

The full book cover image showing the West Branch
of the Penobscot River where it begins at the
Seboomook Dam.

Image Courtesy of Cheryl Derico
(*cderico photography*)

OLD PENOBSCOT STREAM

It was in Bangor City,
In the middle of July,
When five and thirty lumberjacks
Bid their loved ones good bye.
They went to old Seboomook
All feeling pretty mean
And on they went and pitched their tent
    On Old Penobscot Stream.

The work was cutting dry kye,
To clear the right of way;
The hours were long but we were strong
And worked hard day by day.
For eating we had plenty
Of the great and glorious Bean;
And lots of ham, down side the dam
    On Old Penobscot Stream.

The work went rolling nicely
On and on for just a week,
When somewhere in Seboomook
The sky began to leak.
it rained so far we thought at last
The sun would never gleam,
It kept its rays for better days
    On Old Penobscot Stream.

Seboomook was once beautiful,
Its woods and mountains grand,
The fish that were in the river
The best that's in the land.
But now her beauty is all gone
It all seems but a dream,
All that remains is lots of rain
    In Old Penobscot Stream.

The summer days are rolling by
The winter soon will come,
It will make us think of the happy days
We soon will spend at home.
With our fifty bits and both our mits
And a ten spot in between,
With spirits high we'll bid good bye
    To Old Penobscot Stream.

Good bye to old Seboomook,
Good bye to all the rains,
Some day when we get busted
We may come back again.
Our boss has used us very good,
Our cook is a cockareen,
But we'll never forget the boys we met
    On Old Penobscot Stream.

A lumberman's ballad from the early 1900s.
Author unknown

About Tommy Carbone

Tommy Carbone lives in Maine and spends a wicked amount of his time exploring the waterways and trails of the north woods. He writes from a one room cabin, on the shores of a lake, that is frozen for almost six months out of the year, and moose outnumber people three to one.

His first novel, *"The Lobster Lake Bandits – Mystery at Moosehead,"* has made those 'from away' want to visit Maine. It's a big state – come explore.

BOOKS FROM MAINE

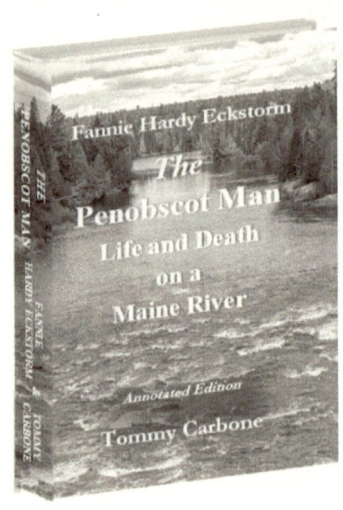

THE PENOBSCOT

MAN

Life and Death

on a

Maine River

A classic book of river-
driver stories from
Fannie Hardy Eckstorm.
Now in an updated and
annotated edition with
never before published
information.

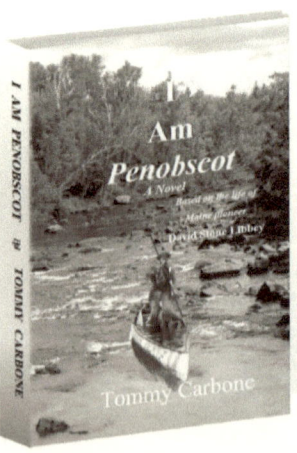

I Am Penobscot

A Novel

If you enjoyed the story
about Maine pioneer
David Stone Libbey, this
historical fiction novel is
sure to entertain the
reader who loves Maine
history and discovering
about American pioneers
and life as a river-driver.

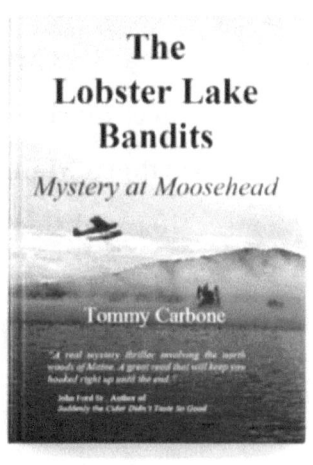

The first novel in the

Moosehead Mystery

series.

Poachers, Game Wardens, and unknown characters roaming the Maine woods make for a suspenseful assignment for New York writer Sarah Molloy.

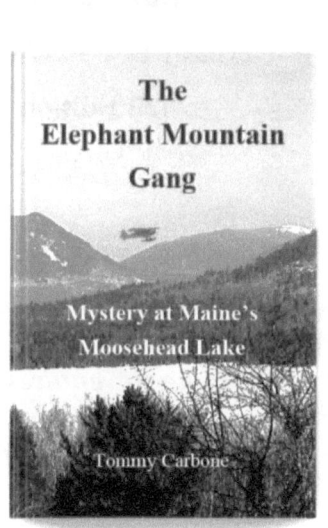

The second novel in the

Moosehead Mystery

series.

Game Warden Henry Ford, Joe Parker, and Sarah get mixed up in a crime that brings to the small town of Greenville a mystery man who may be up to no good.

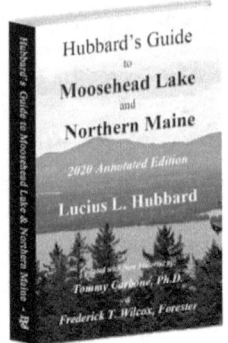

Hubbard's Guide to exploring Northern Maine. 2020 Edition

Hubbard's adventure through Maine to Canada. 2020 Edition

Thomas S. Steele's Maine Adventures.

Two book collection.

Based on the writing of
Fannie Hardy Eckstorm
this memoir is a
wonderful tale of the
Maine woods and history
from the 1800s.

An annotated edition of
stories from:
Fannie Hardy Eckstorm,
Manly Hardy
&
Other writings on Maine.

www.tommycarbone.com